# How to Get Rid of "it"

# Before "it" Gets Rid of You

## Healing and Deliverance from Negative Relationships

## A Practical Self-Help Guide to Spiritual and Personal Growth

*A series of easy spiritual exercises, interactive tools,*
*And step-by-step instructions to receive*
*Freedom from bondage*
*And experience spiritual healing and deliverance*

## Volume Four

**ISBN-13: 978-1986166331**

**ISBN-10: 1986166333**

1

# How to Get Rid of "it"

# Before "it" Gets Rid of You

## Healing and Deliverance from Negative Relationships

## A Practical Self-Help Guide to Spiritual and Personal Growth

*A series of easy spiritual exercises, interactive tools,*
*And step-by-step instructions to receive*
*Freedom from bondage*
*And experience spiritual healing and deliverance*

## Volume Four

**Compilations of Works**
**By**
**Dr. Paulette Douglas**

## DEDICATION

This book is dedicated to my Loving, Supportive, Faithful Best Friend,
Bishop Vanessa Landry, PhD

For the past 28 years, she has inspired me to be the Women that God has ordained me to be
and to continue to minister to God's people and to make full proof of my ministry

# CONTENT

**How to Get Rid of "it", Before "it" Gets Rid of You**

**How to Get Rid of "it", Before "it" Gets Rid of You** is a Deliverance and Spiritual Warfare Manual compiled by Dr. Paulette Douglas which is worth reading and re-reading more than once, in order to empower the reader when confronting personal crisis and trials. Dr. Paulette Douglas has compiled many practical, spiritual books bringing light to the evil that exists. She brings the deliverance ministry to the forefront, explaining how each and every believer can counteract evil and the devil. Not many believers understand the concept of the Holy Spirit and that we are all called to fight against the devil, our enemy. Dr. Paulette Douglas presents scriptural background and Bible passages from the old and new testaments, as well as prayers to share with the reader that each of us is called to resist and fight against the devil with the power of the Holy Spirit. Dr. Paulette Douglas refers to this as the deliverance ministry and explains this is one of the privileges all believers have at our disposal.

This background scripture material is necessary as many readers may be unfamiliar with these spiritual concepts. The main focus on the book is to be a manual; or one stop guide to show the reader what the bible has to say about deliverance as well as to expose the works and deceptions of the devil as well. The cover itself might seem an actual handbook- yet this book is truly a manual for deliverance. This exhaustive book contains too much information to be digested in a single, quick reading. The words contained are life changing. While some traditional readers and those in organized religion may find this book difficult to believe and a bit theatrical, a close-minded attitude is exactly what the devil wants in order to operate.

It is important to keep in mind the charismatic background of Dr. Paulette Douglas is based on the belief of the real workings of the Holy Spirit and the literal belief in modern day spiritual gifts such as tongues and healing. Much of the book is an invaluable resource where Dr. Douglas has taken scriptural truths and prayers and relates them to the modern-day believer to use and apply when facing any trial or work from the enemy. The scriptural references will empower any reader with a quick resource of how to respond in faith to any difficulty- large and small. It is a spiritual self-help book in the fact that it will allow the reader the tools to look within himself/her-self and identify any areas or issues where Satan has his foothold. Not only that it tells the reader how to face and address these issues! For those who are at a loss of how to begin to approach their spiritual problems there are a number of sample prayers applicable to any number of situations. The reader will get the impression as if this book was written for his or her own situation. This is a book to meditate on and use- and is not intended to collect dust on a book shelf. There are eleven sequels to this handbook which address many other issues that just might cover your "it".

In this twelve-book series, How to Get Rid of "it" Before "it" gets Rid of You we discuss evil spirits and how they operate:
1. The Apostolic anointing and ministry
2. How demons enter and oppress people
3. Curses and how to deal with them
4. Breaking bondages
5. Casting out spirits
6. Healing the wounded heart

7. Ungodly beliefs
8. Ministering to people
9. House cleansing
10. Discerning of spirits

In this volume, we deal with the root causes of the "it' of negative relationships and How to get rid of the "it" of negative relationships before it gets rid of you. Negative relationships are something that plagues many people today, whether addiction to food, sex, drugs, alcohol, smoking, spending, masturbation, porn, etc. Some inexperienced deliverance ministers might go after a spirit of negative relationships, which may bring freedom, but often, it doesn't bring lasting freedom. Many times, there is a root that needs to be pulled up, alongside casting out any residing spirits that are holding the person in bondage to the negative relationships. Getting to the root of the negative relationships is the key to bringing a person lasting genuine freedom. I am going to address the most common roots to negative relationships, and hopefully give you an idea of how this bondage works so that you can minister lasting freedom to this type of bondage.

# INTRODUCTION

## "It Is Finished"
## The Words of Victory

"When Jesus therefore had received the vinegar, he said, "It is finished.""—John 19:30
Words of triumph. In His words, "My God, my God, why hast thou forsaken me?" we heard the Savior's cry of desolation. In His words, "I thirst" we listened to His cry of lamentation. Now there falls upon our ears His cry of jubilation— "It is finished." From the words of the victim we turn now to the words of the Victor. The Cross of Christ has two great sides to it: it showed the profound depths of His humiliation, but it also marked the goal of the Incarnation, and further, it told the consummation of His mission, and it forms the basis of our salvation.

It is finished."  What is found in these three words, "It is finished" is wrapped up the Gospel of God. In these words, contained the ground of the believer's assurance. In those words, is discovered the sum of all joy, and the very spirit of all divine consolation. Every" it" that we could ever encounter in our lives was dealt with on the cross therefore; we have the victory through Jesus Christ over any and every "it".

"It is finished." This was not the despairing cry of a helpless martyr. It was not an expression of satisfaction that the termination of His sufferings was now reached. It was not the last gasp of a worn-out life. No, rather was it the declaration on the part of the divine Redeemer that all for which He came from heaven to earth to do, was now done; that all that was needed to reveal the full character of God had now been accomplished; that all that was required by the Law before sinners could be saved, had now been performed—that the full price of our redemption was now paid.

"It is finished." The great purpose of God in the history of man was now accomplished—from the beginning, God's purpose has always been one and indivisible. It had been declared to men in numerous ways: in symbol and type, by mysterious hints and by plain intimations, through Messianic prediction and through didactic declaration. That purpose of God may be summarized thus: to display His grace in the creating of children in His own image and glory. And at the Cross the foundation was laid which was to make this possible and actual.

"It is finished." What was finished? The answer to this question is a very full one, though many excellent expositors have sought to limit the scope of these words and to confine them strictly to a single application. We are told it was the prophecies concerning the sufferings of Jesus which were finished, and that He referred only to this. It is readily granted that the immediate reference was to the Messianic predictions, yet we think there are good and sufficient reasons for not confining our Lord's words here to them. Yea, to us it seems certain that Christ referred specially to His sacrificial work, for all Scripture concerning His suffering and shame was not yet fulfilled. There remained the dismissal of His spirit into the hands of the Father (Psa 31:5); there remained the "piercing" with the spear (Zec 12:10: and note that the word used in Psalm 22:16 for the piercing of His hands and feet—the act of crucifixion—is a different one); there still remained the preserving of His bones unbroken (Psa 34:20), and the burial in the rich man's grave (Isa 53:9).

"It is finished." What was finished? We answer His sacrificial work. It is true there yet remained the act of death itself, which was necessary for the making of atonement. But, as is so often the case here in John's Gospel wherein our text is found (cf. Joh 12:23, 31; 13:31; 16:5; 17:4), the Lord here speaks of the completion of His work. Moreover, it must be remembered that the three hours darkness was already past, the awful cup had already been drained, His precious blood had already been shed, the outpoured wrath of God had already been endured; and these are the primary elements in the making of propitiation. The sacrificial work of Jesus, then, was completed, excepting only the act of death which followed immediately. But, as we shall see, the completing of the sacrificial work made an end of several things.

"It is finished."

1. Here we see the accomplished fulfillment of all the prophecies which had been written of Him here He should die. This is the immediate thought of the context: "When Jesus therefore had received the vinegar, He said, It is finished" (John 19:30). Centuries beforehand, the prophets of God had described step by step the humiliation and suffering which the coming Savior should undergo. One by one these had been fulfilled, wonderfully fulfilled, fulfilled to the very letter. Had prophecy declared that He should be the "woman's seed" (Gen 3:15), then He was "born of a woman" (Gal 4:4). Had prophecy announced that His mother should be a "virgin" (Isa 7:14), then was it literally fulfilled (Mat 1:18). Had prophecy revealed that He should be of the seed of Abraham (Gen 22:18), then mark its fulfillment (Mat 1:1). Had prophecy made it known that He

Prophecy said that He should be named before He was born (Isa 49:1), then so it came to pass (Luke 1:30-31). Had prophecy foretold that He should be born in Bethlehem of Judea (Mic 5:2), then mark how this very village was His birthplace. Had prophecy forewarned that His birth should entail sorrowing for others (Jer 31:15), then behold its tragic fulfillment (Mat 2:14-18). Had prophecy foreshown that the Messiah should appear before the scepter of tribal ascendancy had departed from Judah (Gen 49:10), then so He did, for though the ten tribes were in captivity, Judah was still in the land at the time of His advent. Had prophecy referred to the flight into Egypt and the subsequent return into Palestine, (Hose 11:1 and cf. Isa 49:3, 6), then so it came to pass (Mat 2:1415).

Prophecy made mention of one going before Christ to make ready His way (Mal 3:1), then see its fulfillment in the person of John the Baptist. Had prophecy made it known that at the Messiah's appearing "the eyes of the blind shall be opened, and the ears of the deaf shall be unstopped, then shall the lame man leap as a hart, and the tongue of the dumb sing" (Isa 35:56), then read through the four Gospels and see how blessedly this proved true. Had prophecy spoken of Him as "poor and needy" (Psa 40:17, see beginning of Psalm), then behold Him not having where to lay His head. Had prophecy intimated that He should speak in "parables" (Psa 78:2), then such was frequently His method of teaching. Had prophecy depicted Him stilling the tempest (Psa 107:29), then this is exactly what He did. Had prophecy heralded His "triumphal entry" into Jerusalem (Zec 9:9), then so it came to pass!

Prophecy announced that His person should be despised (Isa 53:3), that He should be rejected by the Jews (Isa 8:14), that He should be "hated without a cause" (Psa 69:4), then sad to say, such was precisely the case. Had prophecy painted the whole picture of His degradation and crucifixion, then was it vividly reproduced. There had been the betrayal by a familiar friend, the forsaking by His disciples, the being led to the slaughter, the being taken to judgment, the appearing of false witnesses against Him, the refusal on His part to make defense, the establishing of His innocence, the unjust condemnation, the sentence of capital punishment passed upon Him, the literal piercing of His hands and feet, the being numbered with transgressors, the mockery of the crowd, the casting lots for His garments—all predicted centuries beforehand, and all fulfilled to the very letter. The last prophecy of all which remained here He committed His Spirit into the hands of His Father, had now been fulfilled. He cried "I thirst," and after the tendering of the vinegar and gall, all was now "accomplished"; and as the Lord Jesus reviewed the entire scope of the prophetic Word and saw its full realization, He cried,

"It is finished"!
It only remains for us to point out that as there was a complete set of prophecies which had to do with the first advent of Jesus, so also is there a complete set of prophecies which have to do with His second advent—the latter as definite, as personal, and as comprehensive in their scope as the former. As then we see the actual fulfillment of those which had to do with His first coming to the earth, we may look forward with absolute confidence and assurance to the fulfillment of those which have to do with His second coming. And, as we have seen that the former set of prophecies were fulfilled literally and personally, so also must we expect the latter set to be. To grant the literal fulfillment of the former, and then to seek to spiritualize and symbolize the latter, is not only grossly inconsistent and illogical, but is highly injurious to us and deeply dishonoring to God and to His Word.

"It is finished."
2. Here we see the completion of His sufferings. But what tongue or pen can describe the sufferings of Jesus? The anguish, physical, mental, and spiritual, which He endured! Appropriately was He designated "the man of sorrows": suffering at the hands of men, at the hands of Satan, and at the hands of God. Pain inflicted upon Him by enemies and friends alike. From the beginning He walked the shadows which the Cross cast His path. "I am afflicted and ready to die from my youth up" (Psa 88:15). What a light this throws on His earlier years! Who can say how much is contained in those words? For us, an impenetrable veil is cast over the future; none of us knows what a day may bring forth.

But Jesus knew the end from the beginning! One has only to read through the Gospels to learn how the awful Cross was ever before Him. At the marriage-feast of Cana, where all was gladness and merriment, He makes solemn reference to "his hour" not yet come. When Nicodemus interviewed Him at night, the Savior referred to the "lifting up of the Son of man." When James and John came to request from Him the two places of honor in His coming kingdom, He made mention of the "cup" which He had to drink, and of the "baptism" wherewith He must be baptized. When Peter confessed that He was the Christ, the Son of the living God, He turned to His disciples and began to show unto them "how that he must go unto Jerusalem, and suffer many things of the elders and chief priests and scribes, and be killed, and be raised again the third day" (Mat 16:21). When Moses and Elijah stood with Him on the Mount of Transfiguration, it was to speak of "his decease which he should accomplish at Jerusalem" (Luke 9:31).

If it is true we are quite unable to estimate the sufferings of Christ due to the anticipation of the Cross, still less can we fathom the dread reality itself. The physical sufferings were excruciating, but even this was as nothing compared with His anguish of soul. To a consideration of these sufferings we have already devoted several paragraphs in previous chapters, yet we make no apology in turning to them again. We cannot contemplate too often what Jesus endured to secure our salvation. The better we are acquainted with His sufferings, and the more frequently we meditate thereon, the warmer will be our love and the deeper our gratitude.
At last the closing hours have come. There had been the terrible experience in Gethsemane followed by the appearing before Caiaphas, before Pilate, before Herod, and back again before Pilate. There had been the scourging and mocking by the brutal soldiers; the journey to Calvary; the fastening of His hands and feet to the cruel tree. There had been the reviling of the priests, the crowd, and the two thieves crucified with Him.

There had been the awful cloud that hid from the Father's face, which wrung from Him the bitter cry, "My God, my God, why hast thou forsaken me?" There had been the parched lips which drew from Him the exclamation "I thirst." There had been the fearful conflict with the power of darkness as the serpent "bruised" His heel. But now the suffering is ended. The Lord has bruised Him; man, and Devil have done their worst. The cup has been drained. The awful storm of God's wrath has spent itself. The darkness is ended. The sword of divine justice is done. The wages of sin have been paid. The prophecies of His sufferings are all fulfilled. The Cross has been "endured." Divine holiness has been fully satisfied (Isa 53:11). With a cry of triumph—a loud cry, a cry which reverberated throughout the entire universe—Jesus exclaims, "It is finished." The shame, the suffering and agony, are past. Never again shall He experience pain. Never again shall He endure the contradiction of sinners against Himself. Never again shall He be in the hands of Satan. Never again shall the light of God's countenance be hidden from Him. Blessed be God, all that is finished! "It is finished."

Jesus is concerned in the work of Redemption: He was the One who came here to die for sinners. He is the One who now gives spiritual illumination and understanding, and guides into the truth. Before the Lord Jesus came to this earth, a definite work was committed to Him. In the volume of the book it was written of Him, and He came to do the recorded will of God. Even as a boy of twelve the "Father's business" was before His heart and occupied His attention. Again, in John 5:36 we find Him saying, "But I have greater witness than that of John: for the works which the Father hath given me to finish, the same works that I do." And on the last night before His death, in that wonderful high priestly prayer, we find Him saying, "I have glorified thee on the earth: I have finished the work which thou gavest me to do" (John 17:4).

The mission upon which God had sent His Son into the world was now accomplished. It was not actually finished till He breathed His last, but death was only an instant ahead, and in anticipation of it He cries "It is finished." The demanding work is done. The divinely-given task is performed. A work more honorable and momentous than ever entrusted to man or angels, has been completed. That for which He had left heaven's glory that for which He had taken upon Him the form of a servant, that for which He had remained upon earth for thirty-three years to do, was now consummated. Nothing remained to be added. The goal of the Incarnation is reached. With what joyous triumph must He here have viewed the costly work which, committed to Him, had now been perfected!

"It is finished." The mission upon which God had sent His Son into the world was accomplished. That which had been eternally purposed had come to pass. The plan of God had been fully carried out.

Because He is the Most High, God's will, cannot be thwarted. Because He is supreme, God's counsel must stand. Because He is almighty, God's purpose cannot be overthrown.
"But he is in one mind, and who can turn him? And what his soul desireth, even that he doeth" (Job 23:13). "I know that thou canst do everything, and that no thought can be withholding from thee" (Job 42:2). "But our God is in the heavens: He hath done whatsoever he hath pleased" (Psa 115:3). "There is no wisdom nor understanding nor counsel against the Lord" (Pro 21:30). "For the Lord of hosts hath purposed, and who shall disannul it? And His hand is stretched out, and who shall turn it back?" (Isa 14:27). "Remember the former things of old: for I am God, and there is none else; I am God, and there is none like me: Declaring the end from the beginning, and from ancient times the things that are not yet done, saying, My counsel shall stand, and I will do all my pleasure" (Isa 46:9-10). "And all the inhabitants of the earth are reputed as nothing: and he doeth according to his will in the army of heaven, and among the inhabitants of the earth: and none can stay his hand, or say unto him, What doest thou?" (Dan 4:35). And, in the triumphant cry of the Jesus— "It is finished"—we have a prophecy and pledge of the ultimate carrying out of God's plan completely. At the end of time, when everything is wound up, and God's purpose has been fully consummated, when everything has been done which He before determined should be done, then shall it be said again, "It is finished."

"It is finished."
4. Here we see the accomplishment of the Atonement. Above we have spoken of Christ reaching the goal of the Incarnation, and of the consummation of His mission to the earth; what that goal and mission was, the Scriptures plainly reveal. The Son of Man came here "to seek and to save that which was lost" (Luke 19:10). Christ Jesus came into the world "to save sinners" (1Ti 1:15). God sent forth His Son, born of a woman, "to redeem them that were under the law" (Gal 4:5). He was manifested "to take away our sins" (1Jo 3:5). And all this involved the Cross. The "lost" which He came to seek could only be found there—in the place of death and under the condemnation of God. Sinners could be "saved" only by One taking their place and bearing their iniquities. They who were under the Law could be "redeemed" only by Another fulfilling its requirements and suffering its curse. Our sins could be "taken away" only by their being blotted out by the precious blood of Christ. The demands of justice must be met; the requirements of God's holiness must be satisfied; the awful debt we incurred must be paid. And on the Cross, this was done; done by none less than the Son of God; done perfectly; done once for all.

"It is finished."
That to which so many types looked forward, was now accomplished. A covering from sin and its shame, typified by the coats of skin with which the Lord God clothed our first parents, was now provided. The more excellent sacrifice, typified by Abel's lamb, had now been offered. A shelter from the storm of divine judgment, typified by the Ark of Noah, was now furnished. The only-begotten and well-beloved Son, typified by Abraham's offering up of Isaac, had already been placed upon the altar. A protection from the avenging angel, typified by the shed blood of the Passover-lamb, was now supplied. A cure from the serpent's bite, typified by the serpent of

brass upon the pole, was now made ready for sinners. The providing of a life-giving fountain, typified by Moses striking the rock, was now affected.

"It is finished." The Greek word here, teleo, is translated variously in the New Testament. A glance at some of the different renderings in other passages will enable us to discern the fullness and finality of the term used by Jesus. In Matthew 11:1, teleo is rendered as follows, "When Jesus had made an end of commanding his twelve disciples, he departed thence." In Matthew 17:24 it is rendered, "They that received tribute money came to Peter, and said, Doth not your master pay tribute?" In Luke 2:39, it is rendered, "And when they had performed all things according to the Law of the Lord, they returned into Galilee." In Luke 18:31, it is rendered, "All things that are written by the prophets concerning the Son shall be accomplished."

"It is finished." He cried: it is "made an end of"; it is "paid"; it is "performed"; it is "accomplished." What was made an end of? —our sins and their guilt. What was "paid?"—the price of our redemption. What was "performed?"—the utmost requirements of the Law. What was "accomplished?"—the work which the Father had given Him to do. What was "finished?"—the making of atonement. God has furnished at least four proofs that Christ did finish the work which was given Him to do. First, in the rending of the veil, which showed that the way to God was now open. Second, in the raising of Christ from the dead, which evidenced that God had accepted His sacrifice. Third, the exaltation of Christ to His own right hand, which demonstrated the value of Christ's work and the Father's delight in His person. Fourth, the sending to earth of the Holy Spirit to apply the virtues and benefits of Christ's atoning death.

"It is finished." What was "finished?"—the work of atonement. What is the value of that to us? This: to the sinner, it is a message of glad tidings. All that a Holy God requires has been done. Nothing is left for the sinner to add. No works from us are demanded as the price of our salvation. All that is necessary for the sinner is to rest now by faith upon what Christ did. "The gift of God is eternal life through Jesus Christ our Lord" (Rom 6:23). To the believer, the knowledge that the atoning work of Christ is finished brings a sweet relief over against all the defects and imperfections of his services. There is nothing "finished" that we do: all our duties are imperfect. There is much of sin and vanity in the very best of our efforts, but the grand relief is that we are "complete" in Christ (Col 2:10)! Christ and His finished work are the ground of all our hopes. "It is finished."

5. Here we see the end of our sins. The sins of the believer, all of them, were transferred to the Jesus. As the Scripture says, "The Lord hath laid on him the iniquities of us all" (Isa 53:6). If then God laid my iniquities on Christ, they are no longer on me. Sin there is in me, for the old Adamic nature remains in the believer till death or till Christ's return, should He come before I die; but there is no sin on me. This distinction between sin in and sin on, is a vital one, and there should be little difficulty in apprehending it. If I were to say the judge passed sentence on a criminal, and that he is now under sentence of death, everyone would understand what I meant. In like manner, everyone out of Christ has the sentence of God's condemnation resting upon him. But when a sinner believes in the Lord Jesus, and receives Him as his Lord and Master, obey the salvation message according to (Acts 2:38-39) he is no longer "under condemnation"— sin is no longer on him, that is, the guilt, the condemnation, the penalty of sin, is no longer upon him. And why? Because Christ bore our sins in His own body on the tree (1Pe 2:24)—the guilt,

condemnation, and penalty of our sins, was transferred to our substitute. Hence, because my sins were transferred to Christ, they are no more upon me.

This precious truth was strikingly illustrated in Old Testament times regarding Israel's annual Day of Atonement. On that day, Aaron, the high priest (a type of Christ), made satisfaction to God for the sins which Israel had committed during the previous year. The way this was done is described in Leviticus 16. Two goats were taken and presented before the Lord at the door of the tabernacle: this was before anything was done with them: it represented Christ being sent and presenting Himself, offering to come into this world and be the Savior of sinners. One of the goats was then taken and killed, and its blood was carried into the tabernacle, within the veil, into the Holy of Holies, and there it was sprinkled before and upon the mercy seat—foreshadowing Christ offering Himself as a sacrifice, to meet the demands of His justice and satisfy the requirements of His holiness.

Then we read that Aaron came out of the tabernacle and laid both his hands upon the head of the second (living) goat— signifying an act of identification by which Aaron is the representative of the whole nation, identified the people with it, acknowledging that its doom was what their sins merited, and which, today, corresponds with the hands of faith laying hold of Christ and identifying ourselves with Him in His Death. Having laid his hands on the head of the live goat, Aaron now confessed over him "all the iniquities of the children of Israel, and all their transgressions in all their sins, putting them upon the head of the goat" (Lev 16:21). Thus, were Israel's sins transferred to their substitute. Finally, we are told, "And the goat shall bear upon him all their iniquities unto a land not inhabited: and he shall let go the goat in the wilderness" (Lev 16:22). The goat bearing Israel's sins, was taken unto an uninhabited wilderness, and the people of God saw him and their sins no more! In type this was Christ taking our sins into that desolate land where God was not and there making an end of them. The Cross of Christ then is the grave of our sins!

"It is finished."
6. Here we see the fulfillment of the Law's requirements. "The law is holy, and the commandment holy, and just and good" (Rom 7:12). How could it be anything less when Jehovah Himself had framed and given it! The fault lay not in the Law but in man who, being depraved and sinful, could not keep it. Yet that Law must be kept, and kept by a man, so that the Law might be honored and magnified, and its giver vindicated. Therefore, we read, "For what the law could not do, in that it was weak through the flesh, God sending his own Son, in the likeness of sinful flesh, and for sin, condemned sin in the flesh: that the righteousness of the law might be fulfilled in [not by] us, who walk not after flesh, but after the Spirit" (Rom 8:3-4). The "weakness" here is that of fallen man. The sending forth of God's Son in the likeness of sin's flesh (Greek) refers to the Incarnation: as we read in another Scripture, "God sent forth his Son, born of a woman, born under the law, that he might redeem them that were under the law" (Gal 4:4-5 RV). Yes, the Jesus was born "under the law," born under it that He might keep it perfectly in thought, word, and deed. "Think not that I am come to destroy the law, or the prophets: I am not come to destroy, but to fulfill" (Mat 5:17); such was His claim.

But not only did Jesus keep the precepts of the Law, He also suffered its penalty and endured its curse. We had broken it, and taking our place, He must receive its just sentence. Having received its penalty and endured its curse, the demands of the Law are fully met, and justice is satisfied. Therefore, is it written of believers, "Christ hath redeemed us from the curse of the law, being made a curse for us" (Gal 3:13). And again, "For Christ is the end of the law for righteousness to everyone that believeth" (Rom 10:4). And yet again, "For ye are not under the law, but under grace" (Rom 6:14). "It is finished." "Free from the Law, Jesus hath bled, and there is remission, cursed by the law and bruised by the fall, Grace hath redeemed us once for all."

7. Here we see the destruction of Satan's power. See it by faith. The Cross sounded the death of the devil's power. To human appearances it looked like the moment of his greatest triumph, yet, it was the hour of his ultimate defeat. In view of the Cross Jesus declared, "Now is the judgment of this world: now shall the prince of this world be cast out" (Joh 12:31). It is true that Satan has not yet been chained and cast into the bottomless pit, nevertheless, sentence has been passed (though not yet executed); his doom is certain; and his power is already broken so far as believers are concerned.

For the Christian, the devil is a vanquished foe. He was defeated by Christ at the Cross— "that through death he might destroy him that had the power of death, that is, the devil" (Hebrew 2:14). Believers have already been "delivered from the power of darkness" and translated into the kingdom of God's dear Son (Col 1:13). Satan, then, should be treated as a defeated enemy. No longer has he any legitimate claim upon us. Once we were his lawful "captives"; but now God worketh in us both to will and to do of His good pleasure. All that we now must do is to "resist the devil," and the promise is, "he will flee from you" (James 4:7).

"It is finished." Here was the triumphant answer to the rage of man and the enmity of Satan. It tells of the perfect work which meets sin in the place of judgment. All was completed just as God would have it, just as the prophets had foretold, just as the Old Testament ceremonial had foreshadowed, just as divine holiness demanded, and just as sinners needed. How strikingly appropriate is this sixth Cross-utterance of Jesus found in John's Gospel—the Gospel which displays the glory of Christ's deity! He seals it with His own words, attesting it is complete, and giving it the all-sufficient sanction of His own approval. Jesus says, "It is finished"—who then dare doubt or question it.

"It is finished." Reader, do you believe it? or, are you trying to add something of your own to the finished work of Christ to secure the favor of God? All you must do is to accept the pardon which He purchased. God is satisfied with His work on the cross, why are not you? Sinner, the moment you believe Jesus' testimony that it is finished, that moment every sin you have committed is blotted out, and you stand accepted in Christ! O would you not like to possess the assurance that there is nothing between your soul and God? Would you not like to know that every sin had been atoned for and put away? Then believe what God's Word says about Christ's death. Rest not on your feelings and experiences but on the written Word. There is only one way of finding peace, deliverance, wholeness, salvation, victory over the "it" and that is through faith in the shed blood of Jesus the of Lamb God.  It is time to "Get Rid of "it", Before "it" Gets Rid of You".

"It is finished." Do you really believe it? Or, are you endeavoring to add something of your own to it and thus merit the favor of God?  By continuing to hold on and struggle, seeking other sources to deal with the "it" in your life, you are nullifying the finished work of Christ by your own miserable additions to it!". The Gospel of God's grace, and the finished work of Christ is sufficient for our souls to rest upon. In the pages of this book, God uses forceful object lessons and His Word to show you, "How to Get Rid of "it", before "it" Gets Rid of You". It is a grave mistake not to embrace the Word of God, and cast yourself by faith upon what Christ had done for you.

Victory was given to us by way of the cross. Whatever your "it" or "its" might be, "it" has come to kill, steal and destroy you. Make a conscious effort to explore this information given in this book and expose the enemy of your soul. Let's "Get Rid of "it". After all, "It is Finished"

## CHAPTER ONE

### What is "it"?

We are all created with a basic need to be loved. God created us to both give and receive love, but though damaged emotions, our capacity to receive love can be dramatically hindered. Ignorance of God's love will also hinder us from receiving the great and glorious love that He has for us. **The root of most "its" is a lack of love being received by that person.** Many of us have been damaged emotionally by rejection, abandonment, abuse, etc., and thereby our capacity to receive love has been reduced. **Only an emotionally healthy person is capable of both giving and receiving love as God intended.**

**Self-worth issues can hinder love**

Self-worth issues are rooted in believing that we are not worthy or deserve to be loved. When we believe that we are unlovable, we will unconsciously reject any love that comes our way. We won't believe the love, because we believe in our hearts that we are not worthy. **Self-worth issues are all rooted in our failing to see who we really are in Christ.**

If you walked into a gallery of world-class art, and pointed to a painting, saying, "That is the ugliest thing I've ever seen! Who painted that??" Now let's say the artist was standing right next to you. How do you think that would make him feel? Do you realize we are the artwork of God, a special painting crafted together by the master painter? Do you think it brings Him honor when we look down on ourselves? **We need to stop putting down what God has made.**

Many times, we have self-unforgiveness issues because we blame ourselves for something, or we've done something we deeply regret, and we simply cannot let it go. We need to realize that Jesus has forgiven us of all our failures, and we need to start seeing ourselves as forgiven. Otherwise, we're denying the work of Christ in our life! **If God forgave you, and you're still beating yourself up, then you don't really believe what Jesus did for you.** It's that simple!

Just as we must forgive others (see Matthew 18:21-35), we need to forgive ourselves just the same. Self-hate has been known to be the root behind diseases such as lupus and Crohn's disease, as well as other auto-immune diseases. We need to stop holding ourselves accountable for that which Jesus has set us free from.

If we want to be in faith, we need to BELIEVE what Jesus did for us, and part of that believing is seeing ourselves as forgiven and clothed with the righteousness of God, which is upon all who believe in the finished work of Christ. Without faith, it is impossible to please God (see Hebrews 11:6), so if you want to please God, start taking the finished work of the cross seriously, and begin to see yourself as forgiven, washed clean, and clothed in the righteousness of God. For the righteousness (right standing with God) is upon all who believe:

*"Even the righteousness of God which is by faith of Jesus Christ unto all and upon all them that believe..." (Romans 3:22 KJV)*

Unforgiveness is rooted in a lack of realization of how much God has forgiven us, and therefore we're not thankful for the steep and terrible price that Jesus paid for our own failures. Therefore, it is so important to mediate on what Jesus did for us, until it transforms our heart. The message of Jesus' work for us is what causes faith to arise in our hearts and transforms us from the inside out (read Romans 10:8-17).

Learning to see yourself as God sees you, and forgive yourself because you want to please God and be in faith and be thankful for what Jesus did for you, is the biggest step in overcoming self-worth issues. Of course, there are spirits that may need to be driven out as well, such as self-hate, guilt, condemnation, etc.

**Receiving the love God has for us**

When it comes to God's love for us, that's obvious, considering how He loves even the sinner so much that Jesus came to die for them. Anybody who knows the message of the cross, has some knowledge of God's love for us. However, many times, we blame God for our problems, and so we don't believe the love that He has for us. Not only do we blame Him for our problems, many times we think that God gave us the sickness or problem in our life to teach us something. Nothing could be further from the truth! Jesus tells us clearly who came to kill, steal, and destroy, and who came so that we could have life and have it in abundance.

*"The thief cometh not, but for to steal, and to kill, and to destroy: I am come that they might have life, and that they might have it more abundantly." (John 10:10 KJV)*

**If we are going to receive the love that God has for us, we need to get our thinking straightened out.** He's not the one behind our problems, but rather Jesus paid the full price so that we can be forgiven all our sins, both physically and emotionally healed, and blessed.

*"When the even was come, they brought unto him many that were possessed with devils: and he cast out the spirits with his word, and healed all that were sick: That it might be fulfilled which was spoken by Esaias the prophet, saying, Himself took our infirmities, and bare our sicknesses." (Matthew 8:16-17 KJV)*

Look at how good God's heart is toward mankind! Not only did Jesus heal them, but He proved the blessings of the covenant we have with Him today concerning our healing and deliverance. Isn't He good toward us? **The reason why things happen to us, is because we live in a fallen world that is under the control of the evil one.** It's not God's fault. He loves you. Jesus died for you.

Settling the fact that God loves you and is good toward you is crucial to restoring your God-given capacity to receive His love. If you can't receive His love, then you need to stop and ask yourself four questions:

1. Am I blaming God for anything bad that happened to me?

2. Have I been emotionally wounded in such a way that it is hindering my ability to freely receive love as God intended me to?

3. Do I have knowledge and revelation of how much God loves me? Do I have a solid Biblical understanding of how I am loved with the same kind of love that the Father has for Jesus?

4. Is there a self-worth issue that makes me feel unworthy to be loved?

Settling these issues lays a foundation for breaking free from the power of the "IT". You must repair the damage and faulty thinking which hinders your ability to receive the love that God has for you.

How do you know if you are receiving God's love or if it's hindered? **If you are not passionate about Jesus, then somewhere your ability to receive His love is hindered.**

If you are living a life without receiving God's love in your heart daily, you are missing out on the most fulfilling life you can have here on this earth. To know God's love, which surpasses all understanding (see Philippians 4:7), dispels all our fears and gives us a sense of peace and joy that we could never otherwise know.

> *"And we have known and believed the love that God hath to us. God is love; and he that dwelleth in love dwelleth in God, and God in him. Herein is our love made perfect, that we may have boldness in the day of judgment: because as he is, so are we in this world. There is no fear in love; but perfect love casteth out fear: because fear hath torment. He that feareth is not made perfect in love." (1 John 4:16-18 KJV)*

**What exactly is "it'?**

An "it" is formed when we try to use something other than God, to meet our need to be loved. When our ability to receive God's love into our hearts is hindered, we will feel like something is missing, and seek to fill that void with something else. When that thing, whatever it might be, fills that void, we grow to love "it" because it's meeting a need. Over time, we establish a relationship with that thing, and when it comes time to depart, it's like breaking up a relationship. That's why the "it" is so destructive; we've relied on that thing to meet a need and we've established a relationship with it. Now when it's time to break up the love, it isn't so easy to say goodbye.

One widespread problem that we see when we try to deal with "it", is where we give up one "it" successfully, only to find yourself with another "it". We might quit drinking only to start overeating, for example. We might think we're finding victory, but all we're really doing is trading one "it" for another "it". This is because something must fill the love-void in our hearts, and if it's not one thing, it will be another.

**What about cutting or self-harm?**

Cutting or self-mutation is a special type of "it", where there's a need to either release pain in a person's heart or the person believes that they deserve to be punished for their failures. In these cases, the person certainly has an issue receiving the love that God has for them but there's another type of root that needs to be addressed as well. There's emotional pain or guilt that the person is dealing with that needs to be resolved. Finding out what happened and receiving Christ's truth concerning those areas is important for their healing. Any bondage involving guilt will need to be resolved through realizing and accepting the work of Christ on the cross for that person and they will likely need spirits of guilt, condemnation, self-hate, etc. driven out in Jesus' name. Again, getting the person to see them self for who they really are in Christ, forgiven, loved, and blessed, is crucial to lasting freedom from self-hate issues.

**See yourself as lovable!**

The key in uprooting most "its" is to deal with the underlying issues which are limiting their capacity to freely receive love from God and others, along with dealing with any self-worth issues by establishing an understanding of your true identity in Christ. **Coming to a place where you believe you are lovable is key to receiving love in general**, so dealing with self-worth issues is an important key to breaking down the walls which keep us from feeling loved. The only way to obtain a true sense of worth and value is to get a revelation of how much you are loved by God, who sent His son Jesus to die for you.

**Discovering the root**

To discover the root of your "it", you need to get real honest with yourself. Many times, we are in denial about the pain we are feeling. Figuring out what is the root of a bondage is all about asking the right questions, and that is especially important when it comes to uprooting an "it". Why don't we feel loved? Do we feel unlovable? (Let's stop right there; if we feel unlovable, then you've just discovered a self-worth issue that will need to be addressed.) Are you passionate about Jesus? If not, then something in hindering you from realizing how much you are loved by Him who died for you. Do you see yourself as forgiven and loved by the God because of what He did for you?

As you discover emotional wounds, you'll need to forgive (others, yourself, and God) and invite Jesus to come and heal the damage in your heart. If you don't realize how much God loves you, then you'll need to spend some time learning about what Jesus did for you on the cross, and what a terrible price He paid because He loved you so very much. Often breaking out of an "it" is a combination of emotional healing, learning about who you are in Christ, forgiving (yourself, others, and God), overcoming self-worth issues by changing how you see yourself (in light of how God sees and loves you), and casting out any spirits that came in and are enforcing the destructive behavior. Spirits behind guilt, condemnation, etc. also need to be driven out, as they seek to keep us from fully seeing what Jesus did for us on the cross.

Dealing with the issues underlying an "it" is key to uprooting it permanently. If you want lasting freedom and wholeness in this area of your life, you will have to deal with the issues that have limited your capacity to receive love, especially the love that God has for you.

**CHAPTER TWO**

**The "it" of Negative Emotions**

**DEFINITION:** Emotions are defined as strong feelings about something or someone.

**FACTS ABOUT EMOTIONS:**

**God created emotions.** God created you in His image and He is an emotional being, expressing emotions such as love, righteous anger, mercy, compassion, etc. As a human being, created in God's image, you also have emotions.

**Emotions can be divided into two categories** A negative emotion is any response that results in adverse thoughts or actions. A positive emotion is any response that results in positive thoughts or actions. There is a broad range of emotions in each of these two categories and a person may also express combinations of these emotional responses. It is your negative emotional responses which you want to eliminate.

**DEALING WITH EMOTIONS:**

**Recognize that negative emotions are powerful.** Unbridled negative emotions can cause you to react in ways that can impact your life forever. Many people who had never violated the law previously are serving lengthy prison sentences because of one violent act done in a fit of anger.

**Understand that negative emotions do not represent the truth.** For example, you may feel fearful when there is nothing to fear. You may worry when in reality; there is nothing about which to be concerned. It is God's Word that speaks the truth into your life, not your own negative emotions or your limited perception of the situations around you.

**Do not try to excuse your negative emotions.** Deal with them, because they are powerful and, left unchecked, they will control your life! You have the power to do so because the Word of God declares that *"You are of God, little children, and have overcome them, because He who is in you is greater than he who is in the world" (1 John 4:4, NKJV).* The same power that raised Jesus from the dead dwells in you and will enable you to control your emotions (Romans 8:11).

**Take responsibility for your emotions.** What negative emotions do you experience and express when you are in difficult situations? Acknowledging these responses will make you more aware of them when they try to surface in your life. Do not blame your emotions on others, i.e., "I'm like my Uncle Jack. I got his temper!" Take responsibility for your own negative responses. You are only responsible for how you react to situations, not for how others respond.

**Make a decision to change.** All change begins with a decision. Your decision to become a believer was the first step toward a new life. Now you must make a decision to allow God to rule in every area of your life, including your emotional responses. You are the only one who can initiate changes in your emotions.  You do this by making a decision to be transformed by the Word instead of being conformed to the world (Romans 12:1-2).

**Realize that you cannot change your nature on your own**.  Self-effort will not rid you of habitual sin. Negative emotions cannot be broken through self-effort.  You must let God supernaturally change your mind, will, and emotions.  For years, your sinful nature has controlled your body and your spirit.  Now you must learn to let your redeemed spirit control your body and soul. Don't give up.  It is a process of spiritual growth.

**Pray about your negative emotions.**  Make your negative emotions a matter of prayer.  God wants you set free from every emotion that has you in bondage.  As you pray about your emotions, God will give you wisdom and power to deal with them.

**Realize that negative emotions call for an immediate response.**  Whenever you recognize a negative emotion beginning to surface, it is a signal that something is wrong.  You need to stop what you are doing, stop what you are saying, or stop what you are thinking.  Do not allow the emotion to be strengthened by your actions, words, or thoughts.  In the name of Jesus and through the power of the Holy Spirit, take control of negative emotions immediately (2 Corinthians 10:4-5).

**Be willing to forgive.**  If you follow the biblical directive to forgive others, many negative emotions will be eliminated.  You have been forgiven by God and people whom you have offended.  Extend this same grace to others

**Wait before you respond.** In difficult situations, think about the response you are about to express.  Is it an attitude that honors God, His Word, and your commitment to Christ?  How does this emotion reflect on you as a believer?  Is it an emotion by which you want to be known?  For example, being angry all the time will make you known as an angry person.

**Take the way of escape.**  Sometimes, you need to remove yourself from a volatile situation or an aggravating person.  God's Word has promised: "*No temptation (trial) has seized you except what is common to man. And God is faithful; he will not let you be tempted (tried) beyond what you can bear. But when you are tempted (tried), he will also provide a way out so that you can stand up under it*" (1 Corinthians 10:13, NIV).  This is God's guarantee that no circumstances, trial, temptation or attack of the enemy will come into your life that you are unable to bear.  In every circumstance you face, God has made a way of escape that will bring you out victoriously.

**Respond as you would like to be responded to.**  Ask yourself how you would like for someone to treat you in a similar situation.  Apply what is called the "golden rule" that is the thesis statement of the Word of God*: "So in everything, do to others what you would have them do to you, for this sums up the Law and the Prophets"* (Matthew 7:12).

**Eliminate volatile situations** when you can do so. This will help, but you may not be able to escape certain people and problems. You can, however, make a decision to change your attitudes and your responses to these circumstances and refuse to respond negatively.

**Avoid toxic people.** Toxic people are those who speak negative things into your life such as "you are stupid, you should be ashamed, you will never amount to anything, etc." Avoiding such people does not give you license to treat them rudely. You can be friendly without being friends. Do not make annoying, insensitive, rude, toxic people your close friends and confidants. Toxic people ignite the sparks of negative emotions in your life. The Bible says: *"Make no friendship with an angry man, and with a furious man do not go, lest you learn his ways and set a snare for your soul" (Proverbs 22:24-25, NKJV).* Substitute any negative emotion for the words "angry" and "furious", and the warning is the same because you learn the ways of those you hang out with. Your own attitudes, actions, and emotions are affected by the company you keep. Make friendships with people who are aggressively following the Lord and will speak the truth of God's Word into your life.

**Don't give up.** If you regress into a negative emotional reaction, do not give up in your quest to eliminate such responses. You never fail until you quit trying! Remember that after your new spiritual birth, your soul–which is your mind, will, and emotions–must be supernaturally changed as you live out this new life. This change is a process of spiritual maturity.

## WHAT GOD'S WORD SAYS ABOUT EMOTIONS:

Here are some general guidelines that are applicable to all negative emotions. For specific emotions, identify the problem and then use a concordance to study all the Bible has to say about it. For example, if you are struggling with anger, commit to memory such verses as: *"A fool gives full vent to his anger, but a wise man keeps himself under control" (Proverbs 19:11).*

So, in everything, do to others what you would have them do to you, for these sums up the Law and the Prophets. (Matthew 7:12)

Do not conform any longer to the pattern of this world, but be transformed by the  renewing of your mind. Then you will be able to test and approve what God's will is his good, pleasing and perfect will.  (Romans 12:1-2).

No temptation (trial) has seized you except what is common to man. And God is faithful; he will not let you be tempted (tried) beyond what you can bear. But when you are tempted (tried), he will also provide a way out so that you can stand up under it. (1 Corinthians 10:13)

The weapons we fight with are not the weapons of the world. On the contrary, they have divine power to demolish strongholds. We demolish arguments and every pretension that sets itself up against the knowledge of God, and we take captive every thought to make it obedient to Christ. (2 Corinthians 10:4-5)

Finally, brothers, whatever is true, whatever is noble, whatever is right, whatever is pure, whatever is lovely, whatever is admirable--if anything is excellent or praiseworthy--think about such things. (Philippians 4:8)

You are of God, little children, and have overcome them, because He who is in you is greater than he who is in the world. (1 John 4:4, NKJV)

**CHAPTER THREE**

**The "it" of Negative Friendship**

**DEFINITION:** Friendship is a relationship of mutual affection between two or more people. It is a strong bond that exceeds a mere association with someone.

**FACTS ABOUT FRIENDSHIP:**

**The two greatest commands in the Bible,** upon which all others depend, are concerned with relationships: *"Jesus replied: 'Love the Lord your God with all your heart and with all your soul and with your entire mind.'  This is the first and greatest commandment.  And the second is like it: 'Love your neighbor as yourself.'  All the Law and the Prophets hang on these two commandments" (Matthew 22:37-40).*  Amazingly, the whole message of the Word of God is summarized in these two commandments--your relationship with God and others!

**There are three basic types of relationships.**

> -A mentor friendship:  This is a relationship in which you are the mentor and you disciple a friend in God's Word and help them grow spiritually.

> -A mentee friendship:  In this relationship, you are the one being mentored by a godly friend who is helping you grow spiritually.

> -A mutual friendship: Mutual friendships are when you are closely aligned with another person on the same spiritual level, and you minister to each other back and forth.

**Do not be unequally yoked in friendship.** The Bible says:  *"Do not be misled: Bad company corrupts good character" (1 Corinthians 15:33).*  We are warned not to be unequally yoked together with unbelievers in any type of relationship (2 Corinthians 6:16).

**Christian friendships are based on Jesus Christ.**  That mutually significant factor provides a sound foundation upon which to build a friendship. He is the one who ..." *...has made both one, and has broken down the middle wall of separation, having abolished in His flesh the enmity, that is, the law of commandments contained in ordinances, so as to create in Himself one new man from the two, thus making peace, and that He might reconcile them both to God in one body through the cross, thereby putting to death the enmity" (Ephesians 2:14-16, NKJV).*

**Christian friends love one another unconditionally**. When difficult times come in the relationship, they continue to love and accept one another despite faults and differences: *"A friend loves at all times, and a brother is born for adversity" (Proverbs 17:17).*  Romans 15:7 indicate that you are to accept others as Christ accepts you--unconditionally.

**Christian friends love sacrificially.**  They are not selfish, rather they give freely of their time, energies, and abilities to their friends: *"Greater love has no one than this that he lay down his life for his friends" (John 15:13).*  Jesus is the best example of a true Christian friend. His love for you is sacrificial, never selfish. He demonstrated this not only through miracles of salvation, healing, and deliverance, but also by the humble service of washing the disciples' feet, and ultimately when He gave His life for you.

**Christian friends do not use one another.** Philippians 2:3 says, *"Do nothing out of selfish ambition or vain conceit, but in humility consider others better than yourselves."* By placing your friend's needs before your own, you will gain a true friend.

**Christian friends edify one another.** "Edification" means to build another person up emotionally, spiritually, and physically. This is done by encouragement based upon God's Word (1 Timothy 5:11).

**Christian friends are honest with one another.** Proverbs 27:6 indicates that *"the wounds of a friend are faithful"*--meaning that even when your friend says something difficult to you that is true, yet painful, they are being a faithful friend. Christian friends can be honest and confront one another when necessary without fearing loss of relationship.

**Christian friends respect confidences.** You are free to share anything with your friend, knowing that it will be kept in confidence.

**Christian friendships are mutually rewarding.** If you feel used, abused, or even smothered in a friendship, something is wrong. Seek to correct it if possible. If not, back off on the relationship.

**Christian friends respect boundaries.** Christian friends will never come between you and God or you and your spouse. They will respect boundaries you set in regards to time spent together and will recognize your need to develop other relationships.

## DEALING WITH FRIENDSHIP:

**Pray about your relationships**. Ask God to bring new friends into your life that will be in harmony with His will and purpose for your life. Ask God for a mentor and ask Him to send people that you can mentor as well. Ask the Lord to show you any negative relationships you might need to sever--people who pull you down or back into the old life.

**Frequent places where you can develop good friends.** Excellent places to find friends are in Church, Bible studies, or prayer groups. If you develop a friend at a local bar, what kind of friend do you think it will be?

**Take the initiative to make friends**. The Bible says: *"A man who has friends must himself be friendly" (Proverbs 18:24, NKJV)*.

**Develop qualities in your life that foster good relationships**. In Galatians 5:16-26 Paul contrasts the qualities of character that result in bad relationships with those that foster good relationships. Attitudes and actions that abort positive relationships are hatred, discord, jealousy, fits of rage, selfish ambition, dissensions, factions and envy. Positive relationships are supported by the Fruit of the Holy Spirit being manifested in your life:  Love, joy, peace, patience, kindness, goodness, faithfulness, gentleness, and self-control.

**Always remember--your friendship with God is most important**.  You cannot be a friend of the world and remain in intimate friendship with God.  (James 4:4)

## WHAT GOD'S WORD SAYS ABOUT FRIENDSHIP

Blessed is the man who does not walk in the counsel of the wicked or stand in the way of sinners or sit in the seat of mockers.  (Psalm 1:1)

A righteous man is cautious in friendship, but the way of the wicked leads them astray. (Proverbs 12:26)

He who walks with the wise grows wise, but a companion of fools suffers harm. (Proverbs 13:20)

A perverse man stirs up dissension, and a gossip separates close friends.  (Proverbs 16:28)

He who covers over an offense promotes love, but whoever repeats the matter separates close friends.  (Proverbs 17:9)

A friend loves at all times, and a brother is born for adversity. (Proverbs 17:17)

A man of many companions may come to ruin, but there is a friend who sticks closer than a brother.  (Proverbs 18:24)

Do not make friends with a hot-tempered man, do not associate with one easily angered, or you may learn his ways and get yourself ensnared. (Proverbs 22:24-25)

Wounds from a friend can be trusted, but an enemy multiplies kisses. (Proverbs 27:6)

Perfume and incense bring joy to the heart, and the pleasantness of one's friend springs from his earnest counsel.  Do not forsake your friend and the friend of your father, and do not go to your brother's house when disaster strikes you.  (Proverbs 27:9-10)

Two are better than one, because they have a good return for their work:  If one falls down, his friend can help him up. But pity the man who falls and has no one to help him up! Also, if two lie down together, they will keep warm. But how can one keep warm alone? Though one may be overpowered, two can defend themselves. A cord of three strands is not quickly broken.  (Ecclesiastes. 4:9-12)

Jesus replied: "'Love the Lord your God with all your heart and with all your soul and with your entire mind.'  This is the first and greatest commandment.  And the second is like it: 'Love your neighbor as yourself.'  All the Law and the Prophets hang on these two commandments."  (Matthew 22:37-40)

Greater love has no one than this that he lay down his life for his friends.  (John 15:13)

Accept one another, then, just as Christ accepted you, in order to bring praise to God
(Romans 15:7)

 Do not be yoked together with unbelievers. For what do righteousness and wickedness have in
common? Or what fellowship can light have with darkness?  What harmony is there between
Christ and Belial? What does a believer have in common with an unbeliever?  What agreement is
there between the temple of God and idols? For we are the temple of the living God. As God, has
said: "I will live with them and walk among them, and I will be their God, and they will be my
people. Therefore, come out from them and be separate, says the Lord.  Touch no unclean thing,
and I will receive you. I will be a Father to you, and you will be my sons and daughters, says the
Lord Almighty."  (1 Corinthians 6:14-18)

Do not be misled: Bad company corrupts good character. (1 Corinthians 15:33)

Do nothing out of selfish ambition or vain conceit, but in humility consider others better than
yourselves.  Each of you should look not only to your own interests, but also to the interests of
others.  (Philippians 2:3)

And the scripture was fulfilled that says, "Abraham believed God, and it was credited to him as
righteousness, and he was called God's friend."  (James 2:23)

You adulterous people, don't you know that friendship with the world is hatred toward God?
Anyone who chooses to be a friend of the world becomes an enemy of God. (James 4:4)

**Do not be friends with:**
    -Gossips: Proverbs 20:19
    -The bad tempered: Proverbs 22:24-25
    -Those given to change: Proverbs 24:21-22
    -Those given to drinking (addiction) and gluttony: Proverbs 23:20-21
    -Liars, untrustworthy, and those who are inconsiderate: Proverbs 25:18-20
    -Those given to violence: Proverbs 1:10-19

**The types of friends to foster.**
    -Those who display wisdom: Proverbs 13:20
    -Those who give wise counsel: Proverbs 27:9; 13:14
    -Those who are comforting instead of dragging you down: Proverbs 17:17 Proverbs
18:24

**Things to avoid in friendships.**
    -Repeating everything you hear: Proverbs 17:9; 26:20
    -Senseless arguments: Proverbs 17:14; 26:21
    -Overstaying your welcome: Proverbs 25:17
    -Bad jokes at the expense of your friend: Proverbs 26:18-19
    -Meddling in affairs that do not concern you: Proverbs 26:17

-Insincere flattery:  Proverbs 27:14
**Solving problems in friendships.**
     -Be slow to anger: Proverbs 16:7
     -Be slow to respond: Proverbs 18:13
     -Avoid quarreling: Proverbs 20:3
     -Speak gently: Proverbs 15:1
     -Speak briefly: Proverbs 10:29
     -Be quick to show love: Proverbs 10:12
     -When necessary, it is better to rebuke than to flatter: Proverbs 28:23.

**The biblical emphasis on relationships** is evident when we note the number of times the words "one another" occurs, particularly in Paul's letters.  We are commanded to:
-love one another: John 13:35
-be devoted to one another: Romans 12:10
-honor others above yourself: Romans 12:10
-live in harmony with one another: Romans 12:16
-comfort one another: 1 Thessalonians 4:18
-encourage one another: Hebrews 3:13
-stir up one another to love and good works: Hebrews 10:24
-show hospitality to one another: 1 Peter 4:9
-employ the gifts of God for the benefit of one another: 1 Peter 4:10
-clothe yourself with humility towards one another: 1 Peter 5:5
-pray for one another: James 5:16
-confess your faults to one another:  James 5:16
-speak to one another with psalms, hymns and spiritual songs: Ephesians 5:19
-submit to one another: Ephesians 5:21, 1 Peter 5:5
-consider others better than yourself: Philippians 2:3
-be concerned about the interests of others: Philippians 2:4
-bear with one another: Colossians 3:13
-teach one another: Colossians 3:16
-build up one another: Romans 14:19; 1 Thessalonians 5:11
-be likeminded towards one another: Romans 15:5
-accept one another unconditionally: Romans 15:7
-admonish one another:  Romans 15:14; Colossians 3:16
-care for one another: 1 Corinthians 12:25
-serve one another: Galatians 5:13
-bear one another's burdens:  Galatians 6:2
-forgive one another: Ephesians 4:2, 32; Colossians 3:13
-be patient with one another: Ephesians 4:2; Colossians 3:13
-be kind and compassionate to one another: Ephesians 4:32

**CHAPTER FOUR**

**The "it" of Enemies**

**DEFINITION:** An enemy is one towards whom you are antagonistic, hostile, and unforgiving. It is someone that you also may be seeking to injure or threaten. You may also try to ruin the reputation of an enemy through slander, gossip, and lies.

**FACTS ABOUT ENEMIES:**

**The Word of God** teaches you not to become bitter, hostile, or vengeful toward another person. You might not like what others do or say, but you must love them and extend forgiveness to them, just as God extended it to you.

**Satan is the source of all contention.** The Bible explains that *"...our struggle is not against flesh and blood, but against the rulers, against the authorities, against the powers of this dark world and against the spiritual forces of evil in the heavenly realms" (Ephesians 6:12).* Your struggle is against the evil forces that cause a person to react in such a way that you consider them an enemy.

**The proper response to contention.** The Fruit of the Holy Spirit, qualities that are to be evident in the lives of believers, provide the answer to contention. *"But the fruit of the Spirit is love, joy, peace, longsuffering, kindness, goodness, faithfulness, gentleness, self-control. Against such there is no law. And those who are Christ's have crucified the flesh with its passions and desires. If we live in the Spirit, let us also walk in the Spirit. Let us not become conceited, provoking one another, envying one another" (Galatians 5:22-23).*

**You are commanded to love and pray for your enemies**. *"You have heard that it was said, 'Love your neighbor and hate your enemy.' But I tell you: Love your enemies and pray for those who persecute you" (Matthew 5:46-47).*

**God can cause your enemies to be at peace with you.** *"When a man's ways are pleasing to the Lord, he makes even his enemies live at peace with him" (Proverbs 16:7).*

**DEALING WITH YOUR ENEMIES:**

**Examine your heart.** If you have hatred, anger, unforgiveness, or bitterness towards someone, then you are not responding biblically to your enemies. Are the feelings and attitudes you have towards this person Christ-like? What caused the break in the relationship? Did you have a part in it? What is the other person's attitude towards you?

**Pray for forgiveness.** Not only for your own attitude towards your enemy, but pray to forgive your enemy also. As a mature believer, the obligation to forgive and initiate reconciliation rests with you. You can do this because the Bible declares you can do all things through Christ (Philippians 4:13).

**Go to your enemy and try to reconcile.**  You cannot control their response, but you can ask forgiveness and seek to reconcile with them.  If they refuse, then you have the satisfaction of knowing you have acted scripturally. Follow the guidelines in Matthew 18:15-17.

**Love and pray for your enemies.**  Jesus commanded this in Matthew 5:43-48.

**Pray for the Fruit of the Spirit** to be manifested in your life towards your enemy:  Love, goodness, kindness, meekness, patience, etc. (Galatians 5:22-23).

**Cast down vain imaginations**.  Vain imaginations are unproductive thoughts and imaginations. When Satan tries to return and instill unforgiveness or bitterness towards the person once again, cast these thoughts down in the name of the Lord (2 Corinthians 10:5).

## WHAT GOD'S WORD SAYS ABOUT ENEMIES:

He is the God who avenges me, who subdues nations under me, who saves me from my enemies. You exalted me above my foes; from violent men you rescued me. (Psalm 18:47-48)

When a man's ways are pleasing to the Lord, he makes even his enemies live at peace with him. (Proverbs 16:7)

Do not gloat when your enemy falls; when he stumbles, do not let your heart rejoice, or the Lord will see and disapprove and turn his wrath away from him.  (Proverbs 24:17-18)

Therefore, if you are offering your gift at the altar and there remember that your brother has something against you, leave your gift there in front of the altar. First go and be reconciled to your brother; then come and offer your gift.  (Matthew 5:23-24)

You have heard that it was said, 'Love your neighbor and hate your enemy.'  But I tell you: Love your enemies and pray for those who persecute you that you may be sons of your Father in heaven. He causes his sun to rise on the evil and the good, and sends rain on the righteous and the unrighteous.  If you love those who love you, what reward will you get? Are not even the tax collectors doing that?  And if you greet only your brothers, what are you doing more than others? Do not even pagans do that?  Be perfect, therefore, as your heavenly Father is perfect.  (Matthew 5:43-48)

For if you forgive men when they sin against you, your heavenly Father will also forgive you. But if you do not forgive men their sins, your Father will not forgive your sins. (Matthew 6:14-15)

So, in everything, do to others what you would have them do to you, for this sums up the Law and the Prophets. (Matthew 7:12)

If your brother sins against you, go and show him his fault, just between the two of you. If he listens to you, you have won your brother over.  But if he will not listen, take one or two others along, so that 'every matter may be established by the testimony of two or three witnesses.'   If he refuses to listen to them, tell it to the church; and if he refuses to listen even to the church, treat him as you would a pagan or a tax collector. (Matthew 18:15-17)

Then Peter came to Jesus and asked, "Lord, how many times shall I forgive my brother when he sins against me? Up to seven times?" Jesus answered, "I tell you, not seven times, but seventy-seven times." (Matthew 18:22-35)

Jesus replied: "'Love the Lord your God with all your heart and with all your soul and with all your mind.  This is the first and greatest commandment.  And the second is like it:  Love your neighbor as yourself."   (Matthew 22:37-39)

And when you stand praying, if you hold anything against anyone, forgive him, so that your Father in heaven may forgive you your sins.  (Mark 11:25,26)

But I tell you who hear me: Love your enemies, do good to those who hate you, bless those who curse you, pray for those who mistreat you.  If someone strikes you on one cheek, turn to him the other also. If someone takes your cloak, do not stop him from taking your tunic.  Give to everyone who asks you, and if anyone takes what belongs to you, do not demand it back.  Do to others as you would have them do to you.  "If you love those who love you, what credit is that to you? Even 'sinners' love those who love them.  And if you do good to those who are good to you, what credit is that to you? Even 'sinners' do that.   And if you lend to those from whom you expect repayment, what credit is that to you? Even 'sinners' lend to 'sinners,' expecting to be repaid in full.  But love your enemies, do good to them, and lend to them without expecting to get anything back. Then your reward will be great, and you will be sons of the Most High, because he is kind to the ungrateful and wicked.  Be merciful, just as your Father is merciful. (Luke 6:27-36)

"So, watch yourselves. If your brother sins, rebuke him, and if he repents, forgive him.  If he sin against you seven times in a day, and seven times comes back to you and says, 'I repent,' forgive him.'"  (Luke 17:3-4)

Bless those who persecute you; bless and do not curse. (Romans 12:14-21)

**CHAPTER FIVE**

**The "it" of Prejudice**

**DEFINITION**:  Prejudice is an unfavorable opinion formed based on insufficient knowledge, inaccurate stereotypes, or irrational feelings.  It is an unfounded hatred, fear, or mistrust of a person or group based on race, nationality, religious, or social status.

**FACTS ABOUT PREJUDICE:**

**Prejudice can take many forms.**  It may appear in how one talks--through slander, criticism, innuendos, or inappropriate racial jokes.  It may also affect one's actions through discrimination, avoidance, cliques, exclusion, abuse, and even murder.

**Prejudice hinders positive relationships**.  It causes you to close your mind and heart towards other people and different people groups.

**Prejudice can be learned**.  For example, if parents are prejudice against a certain race of people by their conversation or actions, they may pass these prejudicial attitudes on to their children.

**Prejudice can be the result of negative experiences**.  For example, a black man who is attacked by a white man, may develop a prejudice against all white people.

**God does not show favoritism**. According to Romans 2:11, God does not show favoritism, nor should we.

**God does not judge by external appearance**. God looks on the heart (1 Samuel 16:7).  He does not judge by external factors (Galatians 2:6).

**DEALING WITH PREJUDICE:**

**Ask forgiveness for your prejudices.**  The Bible says your own judgment or prejudice condemns you: *"You, therefore, have no excuse, you who pass judgment on someone else, for at whatever point you judge the other, you are condemning yourself, because you who pass judgment do the same things" (Romans 2:1).*

**Forgive those who have shown prejudice against you.**  If you have been discriminated against in employment, housing, or personal relationships, forgive the offender.  By forgiving, you are not setting them free from their sinful prejudices, but you are setting yourself free from the effects of it.

**Stop judging by mere appearances** and make a right judgment based on God's Word: *"Stop judging by mere appearances, and make a right judgment" (John 7:24).*

**Accept others as Christ accepts you.**  Accepting others with the same grace and mercy that you are accepted by Christ brings glory to God. (Romans 15:7)

**Make friends among different racial, social, and religious groups.** How can you reach them with the gospel if you are prejudice against them and isolate yourself?

**WHAT GOD'S WORD SAYS ABOUT PREJUDICE:**

Do not mistreat an alien or oppress him. (Exodus 22:21)

But the Lord said to Samuel, "Do not consider his appearance or his height, for I have rejected him. The Lord does not look at the things man looks at. Man looks at the outward appearance, but the Lord looks at the heart." (1 Samuel 16:7)

God does not show favoritism but accepts men from every nation who fear him and do what is right. (Acts 10:34-35)

Stop judging by mere appearances, and make a right judgment. (John 7:24)

You, therefore, have no excuse, you who pass judgment on someone else, for at whatever point you judge the other, you are condemning yourself, because you who pass judgment do the same things. (Romans 2:1)

For God does not show favoritism. (Romans 2:11)

For there is no difference between Jew and Gentile-the same Lord is Lord of all and richly blesses all who call on him, for, 'Everyone who calls on the name of the Lord will be saved." (Romans 10:12-13)

Do not be proud, but be willing to associate with people of low position. Do not be conceited. (Romans 12:16)

Accept one another, then, just as Christ accepted you, in order to bring praise to God. (Romans 15:7)

As for those who seemed to be important--whatever they were makes no difference to me; God does not judge by external appearance (Galatians 2:6)

You are all sons of God through faith in Christ Jesus, for all of you who were baptized into Christ have clothed yourselves with Christ. There is neither Jew nor Greek, slave nor free, male nor female, for you are all one in Christ Jesus. (Galatians 3:26-29)

And masters, treat your slaves in the same way. Do not threaten them, since you know that he who is both their Master and yours is in heaven, and there is no favoritism with him. (Ephesians 6:9)

My brothers, as believers in our glorious Lord Jesus Christ, don't show favoritism.  Suppose a man comes into your meeting wearing some gold ring and fine clothes, and a poor man in shabby clothes also comes in.  If you show special attention to the man wearing fine clothes and say, "Here's a good seat for you," but say to the poor man, "You stand there" or "Sit on the floor by my feet," have you not discriminated among yourselves and become judges with evil thoughts?  Listen, my dear brothers: Has not God chosen those who are poor in the eyes of the world to be rich in faith and to inherit the kingdom he promised those who love him?  But you have insulted the poor. Is it not the rich who are exploiting you? Are they not the ones who are dragging you into court?  Are they not the ones who are slandering the noble name of him to whom you belong?  If you really keep the royal law found in Scripture, "Love your neighbor as yourself," you are doing right.  But if you show favoritism, you sin and are convicted by the law as lawbreakers.  For whoever keeps the whole law and yet stumbles at just one point is guilty of breaking all of it.  For he who said, "Do not commit adultery," also said, "Do not murder." If you do not commit adultery but do commit murder, you have become a lawbreaker. Speak and act as those who are going to be judged by the law that gives freedom, because judgment without mercy will be shown to anyone who has not been merciful. Mercy triumphs over judgment! (James 2:1-12)

## CHAPTER SIX

## The "it" of Judging

**DEFINITION:** Being judgmental or judging is to make and express assumptions about the moral and personal conduct of others.

## FACTS ABOUT JUDGING:

**God is the judge.** God is the judge of us all (Romans 14:12-13). When you take it upon yourself to judge others, you are trying to assume a function of God.

**You will be judged the same way you judge others.** Think about that when tempted to criticize others (Matthew 7:2).

**When you judge others, you condemn your own self.** Very often, you are doing the same things you are criticizing others for--if not worse (Romans 2:1).

**When you judge your leaders, you are criticizing God Himself.** Israel criticized Moses and Aaron, but God viewed it as criticism of Himself because He had set these men in places of leadership (Numbers 14:27).

## DEALING WITH JUDGING:

**Ask God to forgive your judgmental spirit**. Since Jesus said not to judge others, then it is a sin when we do so.

**Focus on dealing with issues in your own life.** Instead of judging and criticizing others, focus on your own moral and spiritual condition (Matthew 7:1-5).

**Ask God to help you guard what you say.** David said, *"Set a guard over my mouth, O Lord, keep watch over the door of my lips" (Psalm 141:3).*

**View others as God sees them.** God sees you and others not as you are, but as you have the potential to become. Look at a person's potential, not their problems.

## WHAT GOD'S WORD SAYS ABOUT JUDGING:

Will not the Judge of all the earth do, right?  (Genesis 18:25b)

Set a guard over my mouth, O Lord; keep watch over the door of my lips. (Psalm 141:3)

Do not judge, and you will not be judged. Do not condemn, and you will not be condemned. (Luke 6:37)

For in the same way you judge others, you will be judged, and with the measure you use, it will be measured to you. Why do you look at the speck of sawdust in your brother's eye and pay no attention to the plank in your own eye? How can you say to your brother, "Let me take the speck out of your eye," when all the time there is a plank in your own eye? You hypocrite, first take the plank out of your own eye, and then you will see clearly to remove the speck from your brother's eye. (Matthew 7:1-5)

And will not God bring about justice for his chosen ones, who cry out to him day and night? Will he keep putting them off? I tell you, he will see that they get justice, and quickly. (Luke 18:7-8)

You judge by human standards; I pass judgment on no one. But if I do judge, my decisions are right, because I am not alone. I stand with the Father, who sent me. (John 8:15-16)

For at whatever point you judge the other, you are condemning yourself, because you who pass judgment do the same things. (Romans 2:1)

So, when you, a mere man, pass judgment on them and yet do the same things, do you think you will escape God's judgment? (Romans 2:3)

Accept him whose faith is weak, without passing judgment on disputable matters. (Romans 14:1)

You, then, why do you judge your brother? Or why do you look down on your brother? For we will all stand before God's judgment seat. (Romans 14:10)

Each of us will give an account of himself to God. Therefore, let us stop passing judgment on one another. (Romans 14:12-13)

The spiritual man makes judgments about all things, but he himself is not subject to any man's judgment. (1 Corinthians 2:15)

I do not even judge myself. My conscience is clear, but that does not make me innocent. It is the Lord who judges me. Therefore, judge nothing before the appointed time; wait till the Lord comes. (1 Corinthians 4:3-5)

Anyone who speaks against his brother or judges him speaks against the law and judges it. When you judge the law, you are not keeping it, but sitting in judgment on it. There is only one Lawgiver and Judge, the one who is able to save and destroy. But you--who are you to judge your neighbor? (James 4:11-12)

**CHAPTER SEVEN**

**The "it" of Envy and Jealously**

**DEFINITION**: Envy is a synonym for jealousy and covetousness excited by the success of others. It is resentment of the spiritual, financial, or material blessings of others. It is lustful desire and longing for something that someone else has. It is sometimes characterized by snide remarks against others in an effort to build up one's own self.

## FACTS ABOUT ENVY AND JEALOUSY:

**Envy comes from the spirit of man.** *"Or do you think Scripture says without reason that the spirit he caused to live in us envies intensely?"* *(James 4:5)*

**Envy is a sign of being a carnal Christian.** *"...for you are still carnal. For where there are envy, strife, and divisions among you, are you not carnal and behaving like mere men?"* *(1 Corinthians 3:3, NKJV)*

**Those living in sin are filled with envy.** *"Being filled with all unrighteousness, fornication, wickedness, covetousness, maliciousness; full of envy, murder, debate, deceit, malignity, whisperers..."* *(Romans 1:29, KJV)*

**Where there is envy, other problems arise.** *"But if you harbor bitter envy and selfish ambition in your hearts, do not boast about it or deny the truth. Such "wisdom" does not come down from heaven but is earthly, unspiritual, of the devil. For where you have envy and selfish ambition, there you find disorder and every evil practice"* *(James 3:14,16).*

**You are not to envy sinners.** *"Do not let your heart envy sinners, but always be zealous for the fear of the Lord"* *(Proverbs 23:17)*

**Envy is a characteristic of false teachers.** *"If anyone teaches false doctrines and does not agree to the sound instruction of our Lord Jesus Christ and to godly teaching, he is conceited and understands nothing. He has an unhealthy interest in controversies and quarrels about words that result in envy, strife, malicious talk, evil suspicions and constant friction between men of corrupt mind, who have been robbed of the truth and who think that godliness is a means to financial gain"* *(1 Timothy 6: -4).*

## DEALING WITH ENVY AND JEALOUSY:

**Acknowledge that you are envious and jealous.** Until you recognize these responses are operating in your life, you will not be able to deal with them.

**Recognize the ramifications of envy and jealousy.** It results in confusion and other evil works (James 3:16) and it ultimately ends in tragedy (Galatians 5:19-21)

**Repent.** Envy and jealousy are sins which require repentance.

37

**Ask God for a new manifestation of His love**. When you truly love someone, you do not envy them, nor are you jealous of them:  *"Love is patient, love is kind. It does not envy..."*
*(1 Corinthians 13:4)*

**In the future:**
> -Walk in the Spirit: Romans 13:13.
> -Manifest the Fruit of the Spirit: Galatians 5:22-23.
> -Focus on things of eternal value instead of things of the world: Colossians 3:1-4.

## WHAT GOD'S WORD SAYS ABOUT ENVY AND JEALOUSY:

A sound heart is the life of the flesh: but envy the rottenness of the bones. (Proverbs 14:30)

Do not let your heart envy sinners, but always be zealous for the fear of the Lord.  (Proverbs 23:17)

Being filled with all unrighteousness, fornication, wickedness, covetousness, maliciousness; full of envy, murder, debate, deceit, malignity, whisperers... (Romans 1:29, KJV)

Let us walk properly, as in the day, not in revelry and drunkenness, not in lewdness and lust, not in strife and envy. (Romans 13:13, NKJV)

...for you are still carnal. For where there are envy, strife, and divisions among you, are you not carnal and behaving like mere men? (1 Corinthians 3:3, NKJV)

Love is patient, love is kind. It does not envy... (1 Corinthians 13:4)

The acts of the sinful nature are obvious: sexual immorality, impurity and debauchery; idolatry and witchcraft; hatred, discord, jealousy, fits of rage, selfish ambition, dissensions, factions and envy; drunkenness, orgies, and the like. I warn you, as I did before, that those who live like this will not inherit the kingdom of God.  But the fruit of the Spirit is love, joy, peace, longsuffering, kindness, goodness, faithfulness, gentleness, self-control. Against such there is no law. And those who are Christ's have crucified the flesh with its passions and desires.  If we live in the Spirit, let us also walk in the Spirit.  Let us not become conceited, provoking one another, envying one another.  (Galatians 5:19-23)

If anyone teaches false doctrines and does not agree to the sound instruction of our Lord Jesus Christ and to godly teaching, he is conceited and understands nothing. He has an unhealthy interest in controversies and quarrels about words that result in envy, strife, malicious talk, evil suspicions and constant friction between men of corrupt mind, who have been robbed of the truth and who think that godliness is a means to financial gain. But godliness with contentment is great gain.  (1 Timothy 6:3-6)

For we ourselves also were sometimes foolish, disobedient, and deceived, serving divers lusts and pleasures, living in malice and envy, hateful, and hating one another.  (Titus 3:3, KJV)

But if you harbor bitter envy and selfish ambition in your hearts, do not boast about it or deny the truth.  Such "wisdom" does not come down from heaven but is earthly, unspiritual, of the devil. For where you have envy and selfish ambition, there you find disorder and every evil practice. (James 3:14,16)

Or do you think Scripture says without reason that the spirit he caused to live in us envies intensely? (James 4:5)

# CHAPTER EIGHT

## The "it" of Disagreements

**DEFINTION**:  To disagree is to have a difference of opinions.  A disagreement is a failure to agree about something.  Unresolved disagreements can lead to arguments, misunderstanding, and disputes.  If resolved biblically, they do not need to do so.

## FACTS ABOUT DISAGREEMENTS:

**People can disagree without having conflict**, but conflict often results from unresolved disagreements.  It is not differences of opinion that hurt and destroy, but the failure to resolve them and to love others despite our differences.

**When people are fighting each other**, they are not fighting the works of Satan or battling for the souls of lost men and women. God wants you to deal with disagreements effectively so the work of His Kingdom can proceed.

**The reasons for conflicts** are detailed in James 3:14-16: *"But if you harbor bitter envy and selfish ambition in your hearts, do not boast about it or deny the truth.  Such wisdom does not come down from heaven but is earthly, unspiritual, of the devil.  For where you have envy and selfish ambition, there you find disorder and every evil practice."*  Again, in James 4:1-3, James declares: *"What causes fights and quarrels among you? Don't they come from your desires that battle within you?  You want something but don't get it. You kill and covet, but you cannot have what you want. You quarrel and fight. You do not have, because you do not ask God.  When you ask, you do not receive, because you ask with wrong motives, that you may spend what you get on your pleasures."*  The Apostle Paul wrote:  *"You are still worldly. For since there is jealousy and quarreling among you, are you not worldly? Are you not acting like mere men?"*
*(1 Corinthians 3:3).*  Remember also that one who is being led by the Spirit will usually come into conflict with others who are being led (at least for a time) by the flesh.

**A good leader** does not ignore disagreements.  He does not call people "unspiritual" for bringing problems to his attention. He immediately deals with disagreements according to scriptural principles.

**Personal disagreements** between believers should not be ignored, but should be resolved according to biblical guidelines.  Do not allow differences of opinion to separate you from other believers or fester in your mind to create anger, bitterness, and unforgiveness.

## DEALING WITH DISAGREEMENTS:

**Prevent conflicts.**  The best way to handle conflict is to prevent it before it occurs.  Here are some ways to prevent conflict:

    -Become spiritually mature (James 3:14-16; 4:1; 1 Corinthians 3:3).

    -Keep others well-informed. Confusion and lack of information often creates problems.

Build strong bridges of communication between those involved with you in the work of the ministry.  Good leaders in the Bible (like Moses, Nehemiah, Ezra, etc.) were good communicators. Communicating with your family is also important.
-We live in an imperfect world.  Expect problems and deal with them immediately when they arise.
-Plan ahead.  By careful planning you can deal with many issues before they become conflicts.  If everyone knows what you are doing and why, there is less opportunity for misunderstanding and conflict.
-Build strong relationships.  It is easier to resolve disagreements when you have a good relationship with others with whom you are interacting.
-If you make a mistake, do not ignore it.  Be big enough to admit and correct it.

**Dealing with conflict.**  When a disagreement arises, follow these guidelines:
-Pray for wisdom to deal with it.
-Determine the real problem.  The conflict is not the real problem.  What caused the conflict is the problem?  To determine the problem you must ask questions, observe, and continue to pray for revelation.  Listen to all sides of the problem and to all people involved.  Do not act without a clear understanding of all the facts.  Always keep in mind the real source of problems (James 3:14-16; 4:1; 1 Corinthians 3:3).
-Let people who are directly affected by the problem suggest solutions. Be willing to      listen to all suggestions.
-Pray together about a solution.  In serious conflicts, fasting is also recommended.
-If the conflict is a personal problem between two people--you and another person--
resolve it according to the principles of Matthew 18:15-17.
-Deal with conflicts with a proper attitude.  Be forgiving, seeking to restore rather than      sever relationships.  Be loving.  Do not threaten or become angry.
-Use tact.  Tact is the ability to deal with difficult situations with wisdom and love without offending people.  It involves being sensitive to others, being understanding, and using words that restore and heal rather than divide and wound.  Be flexible.  Do not be selfishly set on having your own way. Be open to different ideas and ways of solving problems.
-Deal with one conflict or problem at a time.  Do not confuse the issue by discussing      other related problems.
-When you have a clear understanding of the problem causing the conflict, act      immediately to correct it.
-Explain to others involved the reason you are handling the conflict the way you are. For example, in the conflict described in Acts 15, the leaders explained their decision  in detail in writing to those involved (Acts 15).

**Use God's Word to resolve issues.**  God's Word is vital in solving discipline problems and conflicts because: *"All Scripture is God-breathed and is useful for teaching, rebuking, correcting and training in righteousness, so that the man of God may be thoroughly equipped for every good work" (2 Timothy 3:16-17).*  God's Word is effective for discipline, reproof, and correction.

**WHAT GOD'S WORD SAYS ABOUT DISAGREEMENTS:**

How good and pleasant it is when brothers live together in unity!  It is like precious oil poured on the head, running down on the beard, running down on Aaron's beard, down upon the collar of his robes.  It is as if the dew of Hermon were falling on Mount Zion. For there the Lord bestows his blessing, even life forevermore. (Psalm 133)

Reckless words pierce like a sword, but the tongue of the wise brings healing.  (Proverbs 12:18)

A gentle answer turns away wrath, but a harsh word stirs up anger.  (Proverbs 15:1)

He who covers over an offense promotes love, but whoever repeats the matter separates close friends.  (Proverbs 17:9)

Where there is no wood, the fire goes out; And where there is no talebearer, strife ceases. As charcoal is to burning coals, and wood to fire, so is a contentious man to kindle strife. The words of a talebearer are like tasty trifles, and they go down into the inmost body. (Proverbs 26:20-22)

For as churning the milk produces butter, and as twisting the nose produces blood, so stirring up anger produces strife.  (Proverbs 30:33)

Do two walk together unless they have agreed to do so?  (Amos 3:3)

Blessed are the peacemakers, for they shall be called sons of God.  (Matthew 5:9)

For if you forgive men when they sin against you, your heavenly Father will also forgive you. But if you do not forgive men their sins, your Father will not forgive your sins.  (Matt. 6:14-15)

If your brother sins against you, go and show him his fault, just between the two of you. If he listens to you, you have won your brother over.  But if he will not listen, take one or two others along, so that every matter may be established by the testimony of two or three witnesses. If he refuses to listen to them, tell it to the church; and if he refuses to listen even to the church, treat him as you would a pagan or a tax collector. (Matthew 18:15-17)

Do not take revenge, my friends, but leave room for God's wrath, for it is written: "It is mine to avenge; I will repay," says the Lord.  On the contrary: If your enemy is hungry, feed him; if he is thirsty, give him something to drink. In doing this, you will heap burning coals on his head.  Do not be overcome by evil, but overcome evil with good. (Romans 12:19)

I appeal to you, brothers, in the name of our Lord Jesus Christ, that all of you agree with one another so that there may be no divisions among you and that you may be perfectly united in mind and thought. (1 Corinthians 1:10)

You are still worldly. For since there is jealousy and quarreling among you, are you not worldly? Are you not acting like mere men?  (1 Corinthians 3:3).

If any of you has a dispute with another, dare he take it before the ungodly for judgment instead of before the saints?  Do you not know that the saints will judge the world? And if you are to judge the world, are you not competent to judge trivial cases?  Do you not know that we will judge angels? How much more the things of this life!  Therefore, if you have disputes about such matters, appoint as judges even men of little account in the church!  I say this to shame you. Is it possible that there is nobody among you wise enough to judge a dispute between believers?  But instead, one brother goes to law against another--and this in front of unbelievers! The very fact that you have lawsuits among you means you have been completely defeated already. Why not rather be wronged? Why not rather be cheated?  Instead, you yourselves cheat and do wrong, and you do this to your brothers. (1 Corinthians 6:1-8)

Make every effort to keep the unity of the Spirit through the bond of peace. There is one body and one Spirit--just as you were called to one hope when you were called--one Lord, one faith, one baptism; one God and Father of all, who is over all and through all and in all.  (Ephesians 4:3-6)

It was he who gave some to be apostles, some to be prophets, some to be evangelists, and some to be pastors and teachers, to prepare God's people for works of service, so that the body of Christ may be built up until we all reach unity in the faith and in the knowledge of the Son of God and become mature, attaining to the whole measure of the fullness of Christ.  (Ephesians 4:11-13)

Be kind and compassionate to one another, forgiving each other, just as in Christ God forgave you.  (Ephesians 4:32)

Do everything without complaining or arguing, so that you may become blameless and pure, children of God without fault in a crooked and depraved generation, in which you shine like stars in the universe as you hold out the word of life. (Philippians 2:14-16)

But now you must rid yourselves of all such things as these: anger, rage, malice, slander, and filthy language from your lips. (Colossians 3:8)

Bear with each other and forgive whatever grievances you may have against one another. Forgive as the Lord forgave you.  And over all these virtues put on love, which binds them all together in perfect unity.  (Colossians 3:13-14)

If anyone teaches false doctrines and does not agree to the sound instruction of our Lord Jesus Christ and to godly teaching, he is conceited and understands nothing. He has an unhealthy interest in controversies and quarrels about words that result in envy, strife, malicious talk, evil suspicions and constant friction between men of corrupt mind, who have been robbed of the truth and who think that godliness is a means to financial gain.  (1 Timothy 6:3-5)

Don't have anything to do with foolish and stupid arguments, because you know they produce quarrels. And the Lord's servant must not quarrel; instead, he must be kind to everyone, able to teach, not resentful. (2 Timothy 2:23-24)

All Scripture is God-breathed and is useful for teaching, rebuking, correcting and training in righteousness, so that the man of God may be thoroughly equipped for every good work.  (2 Timothy 3:16-17).

But avoid foolish controversies and genealogies and arguments and quarrels about the law, because these are unprofitable and useless.  Warn a divisive person once, and then warn him a second time. After that, have nothing to do with him.  You may be sure that such a man is warped and sinful; he is self-condemned.  (Titus 3:9-11)

My dear brothers, take note of this: Everyone should be quick to listen, slow to speak and slow to become angry, for man's anger does not bring about the righteous life that God desires.  (James 1:19-20)

But if you harbor bitter envy and selfish ambition in your hearts, do not boast about it or deny the truth.  Such "wisdom" does not come down from heaven but is earthly, unspiritual, of the devil.  For where you have envy and selfish ambition, there you find disorder and every evil practice.  But the wisdom that comes from heaven is first of all pure; then peace-loving, considerate, submissive, full of mercy and good fruit, impartial and sincere.  Peacemakers who sow in peace raise a harvest of righteousness. (James 3:14-18)

What causes fights and quarrels among you? Don't they come from your desires that battle within you?  You want something but don't get it. You kill and covet, but you cannot have what you want. You quarrel and fight. You do not have, because you do not ask God.  When you ask, you do not receive, because you ask with wrong motives, that you may spend what you get on your pleasures.  (James 4:1-3)

Finally, all of you, live in harmony with one another; be sympathetic, love as brothers, be compassionate and humble.  Do not repay evil with evil or insult with insult, but with blessing, because to this you were called so that you may inherit a blessing.  For, Whoever would love life and see good days must keep his tongue from evil and his lips from deceitful speech.  He must turn from evil and do good; he must seek peace and pursue it.  (1 Peter 3:8-11)

Dear children, let us not love with words or tongue but with actions and in truth. (1 John 3:18)

**Biblical examples of resolving disagreements.**

**Abraham.**  Abraham resolved disagreements between his servants and those of Lot by suggesting they separate and giving Lot the choice of lands (Genesis 13:5-13).

**Paul and Barnabas**.  Paul and Barnabas disagreed over taking a young man named John Mark with them on a missions trip.  The problem was solved by forming a second evangelistic team.  This solution actually advanced the spread of the Gospel.  Paul and Barnabas did not get angry, stop speaking, and have nothing more to do with one another.  Neither one dropped out of Christian service because "someone had hurt them." They both continued on to serve the Lord.  Sometime later, Paul admitted that John Mark--having been trained by Barnabas--was ready for ministry and asked that John Mark be sent to him (Acts 15:36-41).

**The early church.**  Any time a church, an organization, or work of God is launched, it goes through certain stages of development.   Read the following chapters in your Bible:

| | |
|---|---|
| Acts 1 | God chose certain men. |
| Acts 2 | He gave these men a ministry. |
| Acts 3 | There was great multiplication. |
| Acts 4 | A great movement was born (the Church). |
| Acts 5-6 | Persecution and conflict arose. |

In Acts 1-4 a great work of God is birthed, then in Acts 5:1-11, a problem arises.  Peter does not ignore it, but confronts and deals with it.  In Acts 5:12-42, conflict from without the Church arises. The disciples stand in the face of opposition and boldly declare that they should obey God rather than man (Acts 5:29 and 42).  In Acts 6:1, conflict from within the church arises.  There is a dispute over the distribution of supplies to widows.  Again, the disciples immediately solve the conflict (Acts 6:2-7.)  Anytime a ministry or work of God is launched, it will experience a similar pattern.  As it grows, there will be disagreements and conflicts from without and within the fellowship that must be resolved biblically.

**CHARTER NINE**

**The "it of Vengeance
(Retribution and Revenge)**

**DEFINITION:** Vengeance--retribution or revenge--is the infliction of injury, harm, humiliation or punishment in return for an injury or offence.

**FACTS ABOUT VENGEANCE:**

**God forbids revenge.** *"Do not seek revenge or bear a grudge against one of your people, but love your neighbor as yourself. I am the Lord" (Leviticus 19:18).*

**Vengeance is God's responsibility**. It is a function that God alone is to execute (Romans 12:19). When you take matters into your own hands and seek retribution, you are trying to assume God's authority.

**Revenge does not bring closure.** It does not help you forget the wrong you suffered and it does not help you heal emotionally or spiritually. True healing from wrongs suffered cannot be attained when you are violating God's Word by seeking or executing revenge.

**You are to love your enemies.** God's strategy for dealing with someone who wrongs you is to show them love and compassion (Luke 6:27) and seek to resolve offences (Matthew 18:15-16).

**DEALING WITH VENGEANCE:**

**Ask God for forgiveness.** If you have had vengeful thoughts, sought, or taken revenge, ask God to forgive you because you have violated His Word.

**Ask God to give you love for the offender.** This is not something you can generate on your own. It comes through God's power and the Holy Spirit being manifested in your life.

**If you have taken revenge, seek forgiveness.** Ask the one upon whom you took revenge to forgive you. Follow the guidelines of Matthew 18:15-16.

**WHAT GOD'S WORD SAYS ABOUT VENGEANCE:**

Do not seek revenge or bear a grudge against one of your people, but love your neighbor as yourself. I am the Lord. (Leviticus 19:18)

Do not say, "I'll pay you back for this wrong!" Wait for the Lord, and he will deliver you. (Proverbs 20:22)

Do not gloat when your enemy falls; when he stumbles, do not let your heart rejoice. (Proverbs 24:17)

If your enemy is hungry, give him food to eat; if he is thirsty, give him water to drink. In doing this, you will heap burning coals on his head and the Lord will reward you. (Proverbs 25:21-22)

You have heard that it was said, "Eye for eye, and tooth for tooth." But I tell you, do not resist an evil person. If someone strikes you on the right cheek, turn to him the other also. (Matthew 5:38-39)

If your brother sins against you, go and show him his fault, just between the two of you. If he listens to you, you have won your brother over.  But if he will not listen, take one or two others along, so that every matter may be established by the testimony of two or three witnesses.  If he refuses to listen to them, tell it to the church; and if he refuses to listen to the church, treat him as you would a pagan or a tax collector. (Matthew 18:15-17)

Love your enemies, do good to those who hate you. (Luke 6:27)

Do to others as you would have them do to you. (Luke 6:31)

Do not take revenge, my friends, but leave room for God's wrath, for it is written: "It is mine to avenge; I will repay," says the Lord. (Romans 12:19)

Make sure that nobody pays back wrong for wrong, but always try to be kind to each other and to everyone else. (1 Thessalonians 5:15)

Do not repay evil with evil or insult with insult, but with blessing, because to this you were called so that you may inherit a blessing. (1 Peter 3:9)

When they hurled their insults at him *(Jesus),* he did not retaliate; when he suffered, he made no threats. Instead, he entrusted himself to him who judges justly. (1 Peter 2:23)

**CHAPTER TEN**

**The "it" of Injustice**

**DEFINITION:**  Justice is fairness in protection of rights and the punishment of wrongs.

**FACTS ABOUT JUSTICE:**

**Most legal systems aim to uphold the ideal of justice** through proper administration of the laws of their land.  It is possible, however, to have unjust laws and miscarriages of justice.

**Injustices occur because we live in a sinful world.**  No one is perfect--this includes law enforcement officers, judges, juries, and courts involved in the legal system.  Injustices also occur in business dealings and personal relationships.

**Injustice breeds further injustice.**  *"Because the sentence against an evil work is not executed speedily, therefore the heart of the sons of men is fully set in them to do evil"  (Ecclesiastes 8:11, NKJV).*

**Justice is not always fairly dispensed**.  Injustices are often experienced by people without funds for proper representation in a court of law or a business transaction.  Injustices sometimes occur because of race or religious beliefs.

**God is a God of justice.**  He keeps perfect records.  Although someone may escape justice in this world, he will not escape in the world to come unless he repents and comes to Jesus Christ.

**Our standard of justice is the Word of God.**  We are citizens of the Kingdom of God, and we are governed by the mandates of the Word.

**DEALING WITH JUSTICE:**

**Look to God for justice.** God is a righteous judge and the true judge of us all (Romans 14:12-13).  Look to God for justice instead of man (Psalm 140:12).

**Do not seek revenge.**  Do not seek revenge for injustices committed against you.  The Bible says that God forbids revenge (Leviticus 19:18).  Vengeance for injustice is God's responsibility (Romans 12:19).

**Love your enemies.**  God's strategy for dealing with someone who commits an injustice against you is to show them love and compassion (Luke 6:27)

**Seek to resolve offences**.  To the best of your ability, try to resolve offenses that cause injustices and set right any wrongs.

**WHAT GOD'S WORD SAYS ABOUT JUSTICE:**

Will not the Judge of all the earth do right?  (Genesis 18:25b)

Do not pervert justice; do not show partiality to the poor or favoritism to the great, but judge your neighbor fairly.  (Leviticus 19:15)

Do not seek revenge or bear a grudge against one of your people, but love your neighbor as yourself. I am the Lord.  (Leviticus 19:18)

Follow justice and justice alone, so that you may live and possess the land the Lord your God is giving you.  (Deuteronomy 16:20)

Cursed is the man who withholds justice from the alien, the fatherless or the widow.   Then all the people shall say, "Amen!" (Deuteronomy 27:19)

 I thought in my heart, "God will bring to judgment both the righteous and the wicked, for there will be a time for every activity, a time for every deed." (Ecclesiastes 3:17)

 The Lord works righteousness and justice for all the oppressed.  (Psalm 103:6)

I know that the Lord will maintain the cause of the afflicted, And justice for the poor. (Psalm 140:12)

Do not say, "I'll pay you back for this wrong!" Wait for the Lord, and he will deliver you. (Proverbs 20:22)

Evil men do not understand justice, but those who seek the Lord understand all.  (Proverbs 28:5, NKJV)

The righteous considers the cause of the poor, But the wicked does not understand such knowledge.  (Proverbs 29:7, NKJV)

Because the sentence against an evil work is not executed speedily, therefore the heart of the sons of men is fully set in them to do evil.   (Ecclesiastes 8:11, NKJV)

 Learn to do good; Seek justice, Rebuke the oppressor; Defend the fatherless, Plead for the widow.  (Isaiah 1:17, NKJV)

Yet the Lord longs to be gracious to you; he rises to show you compassion. For the Lord is a God of justice. Blessed are all who wait for him!  (Isaiah 30:18)

Listen to me, my people; hear me, my nation: The law will go out from me; my justice will become a light to the nations.  (Isaiah 51:4)

For I, the Lord, love justice; I hate robbery and iniquity. (Isaiah 61:8)

He has showed you, O man, what is good.  And what does the Lord require of you?  To act justly and to love mercy and to walk humbly with your God.  (Micah 6:8)

This is what the Lord Almighty says: "Administer true justice; show mercy and compassion to one another. Do not oppress the widow or the fatherless, the alien or the poor. In your hearts do not think evil of each other." (Zechariah 7:9-10)

And will not God bring about justice for his chosen ones, who cry out to him day and night? Will he keep putting them off? I tell you, he will see that they get justice, and quickly. (Luke 18:7-8)

You judge by human standards; I pass judgment on no one. But if I do judge, my decisions are right, because I am not alone. I stand with the Father, who sent me. (John 8:15-16)

Do not take revenge, my friends, but leave room for God's wrath, for it is written: "It is mine to avenge; I will repay," says the Lord. (Romans 12:19)

Do not repay evil with evil or insult with insult, but with blessing, because to this you were called so that you may inherit a blessing. (1 Peter 3:9)

## CHAPTER ELEVEN

## The "it" of Rejection and Abandonment

**DEFINITION:** The original meaning of the word rejection was to throw back. Rejection occurs when a person or group of people excludes an individual and refuses to acknowledge or accept them. Abandonment is a similar term, meaning to desert someone, to leave and never return.

**FACTS ABOUT REJECTION AND ABANDONMENT:**

**Rejection takes many forms.** It may occur through the ending of a relationship, unrequited affection for someone, losing a job, or through criticism. Feelings of rejection also can arise from emotional or physical abandonment by friends or family or close relations such as a parent or a spouse. Failure to achieve a goal like being accepted by a college or hired for a job can also cause feelings of rejection.

**Reactions to rejection** may include disappointment, anger, sadness, depression, and feelings of isolation and abandonment. Rejection may cause you to stop trying because of fear of rejection. You may experience feelings of inferiority and develop a critical spirit towards yourself or those by whom you were rejected. You may have difficulty in forming relationships because of rejections experienced in the past. Feelings of rejection can actually cause you to miss God's plan for your life when you withdraw to nurse your wounds.

**You are not alone in your rejection**. Many people in the Bible experienced rejection. The Old Testament prophets were often rejected and disrespected. They ended up in lions' dens, pits, and were martyred. Joseph, whose story is recorded in Genesis, was rejected by his family and his brothers sold him into slavery. Moses experienced repeated rejection before Pharaoh. In the New Testament, the Apostle Paul was stoned by one group of people, run out of town, and escaped with his life by being let over the wall in a basket. Peter and John were imprisoned and Stephen experienced the ultimate rejection--he was martyred after preaching one of the greatest messages recorded in the New Testament. Everyone experiences rejection. It is impossible to go through life without feeling rejected at some time.

**God experienced rejection.** In Numbers 14:11 the Lord asked Moses: *"How long will these people reject me? How long will they not believe me, with all the signs which I have performed among them" (Numbers 14:11, NKJV).*

**Jesus experienced rejection.** The prophet Isaiah said concerning Jesus: *"He was despised and rejected by men, a man of sorrows, and familiar with suffering. Like one from whom men hide their faces he was despised, and we esteemed him not" (Isaiah 53:3).* Jesus came to His own people and they rejected him (John 1:11) and He was rejected in His own hometown (Mark 6:4). Like Jesus, you will be rejected because you are not of this world (John 15:18-19).

## DEALING WITH REJECTION AND ABANDONMENT:

**Pray about your rejection issues.** Turn your disappointment, hurt, anger, sadness, depression over to the Lord. Ask Him to heal your wounded emotions. The Bible directs us to give thanks in everything, so thank God that He is guiding your life, even though the pain of rejection and abandonment.

**Determine that you will live by faith.** Rejection is a feeling, but we do not live the Christian life on the basis of feelings. We live by faith in God. We do not live in the natural. We live in the supernatural.

**Permit the power of the Holy Spirit to work in your life**. As a born-again believer, the Holy Spirit dwells within you. Just because you feel rejected, you are not incompetent. You are fully equipped, through the power of the Holy Spirit, to accomplish all that God has called you to do: *"I can do everything through him who gives me strength" (Philippians 4:13).*

**Know that you are who God says you are.** Regardless of what others think about you, as a believer you are who the Lord says you are. You belong to the family of God (Romans 8:16). You are so valuable that Jesus died for you (John 3:16).

**Know that you are really never alone.** Jesus said *"And I will ask the Father, and he will give you another Counselor to be with you forever--the Spirit of truth. The world cannot accept him, because it neither sees him nor knows him. But you know him, for he lives with you and will be in you. I will not leave you as orphans; I will come to you" (John 14:16-18).*

**Do not view rejection as a negative thing.** If you have made Jesus the Lord of your life, then He is guiding each aspect of your life. The fact that you are rejected by a person, group, job, college, etc., may be part of His plan for you. God guides us through closed doors as well as open doors. The Bible says that "all things" work together for your good when you are a true believer who loves God: *"And we know that in all things God works for the good of those who love him, who have been called according to his purpose" (Romans 8:28).*

**Use rejection as a cause to examine yourself.** Honestly assess your actions, attitudes, and responses to others to see if there is a legitimate reason for being rejected. For example, if you were rejected for a job was it because you did not interview well? If you are repeatedly rejected by others, could there be reasons? If you discover legitimate reasons for rejection in any area, correct these with the help of the Lord.

**Do not let rejection hinder you from fulfilling your destiny**. God has a plan for your life. Perhaps rejection has blocked the way you were planning to go, but if your goals and purposes are God-given, you will still achieve them--perhaps just not in the way you thought. Do not let rejection stand in your way. Get up and try again. You never truly fail unless you stop trying, and it is always too soon to quit!

**Overcome your fear of rejection by putting God first.**  When the disciples were imprisoned and threatened by the authorities because of their stand for the Gospel, they declared: *"We must obey God rather than men" (Acts 5:29).*

## WHAT GOD'S WORD SAYS ABOUT REJECTION AND ABANDONMENT:

Read the story of the woman at the well in John chapter 4.  Because of her lifestyle, this woman had obviously been rejected by society, as she came to draw water when no one else was there-- perhaps to avoid the feelings of rejection and the gossip.  Jesus accepted her as she was and changed her life.  She overcame her feeling of rejection and became a powerful evangelist--she brought the whole city out to meet Jesus.

... for you are a people holy to the Lord your God. Out of all the peoples on the face of the earth, the Lord has chosen you to be his treasured possession. (Deuteronomy 14:2)

How long will these people reject me?  How long will they not believe me, with all the signs which I have performed among them?  (Numbers 14:11, NKJV).

The Lord is close to the brokenhearted and saves those who are crushed in spirit. (Psalm 34:17)

For the Lord will not reject his people; he will never forsake his inheritance. (Psalm 94:14)

The stone which the builders refused is become the head stone of the corner. This is the Lord's doing; it is marvelous in our eyes. (Psalm 118:22)

For you created my inmost being; you knit me together in my mother's womb.  I praise you because I am fearfully and wonderfully made; your works are wonderful, I know that full well. My frame was not hidden from you when I was made in the secret place. When I was woven together in the depths of the earth, your eyes saw my unformed body. All the days ordained for me were written in your book before one of them came to be.  (Psalm 139:13-16)

I took you from the ends of the earth, from its farthest corners I called you. I said, 'You are my servant'; I have chosen you and have not rejected you.  So, do not fear, for I am with you; do not be dismayed, for I am your God. I will strengthen you and help you; I will uphold you with my righteous right hand.  (Isaiah 41:9-10)

Can a mother forget the baby at her breast and have no compassion on the child she has borne? Though she may forget, I will not forget you!   See, I have engraved you on the palms of my hands; your walls are ever before me. (Isaiah 49:15-16)

He was despised and rejected by men, a man of sorrows, and familiar with suffering. Like one from whom men hide their faces he was despised, and we esteemed him not.  (Isaiah 53:3)

Blessed are you when people insult you, persecute you and falsely say all kinds of evil against you because of me.  Rejoice and be glad, because great is your reward in heaven, for in the same way they persecuted the prophets who were before you. (Matthew 5:11-12)

Come to me, all you who are weary and burdened, and I will give you rest.  Take my yoke upon you and learn from me, for I am gentle and humble in heart, and you will find rest for your souls. For my yoke is easy and my burden is light. (Matthew 11:28-30)

Jesus said to them, "Have you never read in the Scriptures: 'The stone the builders rejected has become the capstone; the Lord has done this, and it is marvelous in our eyes'? " (Matthew 21:42)

And surely, I am with you always, to the very end of the age. (Matthew 28:20)

Jesus said to them, "Only in his hometown, among his relatives and in his own house is a prophet without honor."  He could not do any miracles there, except lay his hands on a few sick people and heal them.  And he was amazed at their lack of faith.  (Mark 6:4-6)

He who listens to you listens to me; he who rejects you rejects me; but he who rejects me rejects him who sent me. (Luke 10:16)

O Jerusalem, Jerusalem, you who kill the prophets and stone those sent to you, how often I have longed to gather your children together, as a hen gathers her chicks under her wings, but you were not willing!  Look, your house is left to you desolate. I tell you, you will not see me again until you say, 'Blessed is he who comes in the name of the Lord.'  (Luke 13:34-35)

He was in the world, and though the world was made through him, the world did not recognize him.  He came to that which was his own, but his own did not receive him.  Yet to all who received him, to those who believed in his name, he gave the right to become children of God-- children born not of natural descent, nor of human decision or a husband's will, but born of God. (John 1:10-131)

And I will ask the Father, and he will give you another Counselor to be with you forever--the Spirit of truth. The world cannot accept him, because it neither sees him nor knows him. But you know him, for he lives with you and will be in you.  I will not leave you as orphans; I will come to you.  (John 14:16-18)

If you belonged to the world, it would love you as its own. As it is, you do not belong to the world, but I have chosen you out of the world. That is why the world hates you.  (John 15:18-19)

We must obey God rather than men.  (Acts 5:29)

The Spirit himself testifies with our spirit that we are God's children.  Now if we are children, then we are heirs--heirs of God and co-heirs with Christ, if indeed we share in his sufferings in order that we may also share in his glory. (Romans 8:16-17)

And we know that in all things God works for the good of those who love him, who have been called according to his purpose. (Romans 8:28)

Don't you know that you yourselves are God's temple and that God's Spirit lives in you?  If anyone destroys God's temple, God will destroy him; for God's temple is sacred, and you are that temple.  (1 Corinthians 3:16)

Praise be to the God and Father of our Lord Jesus Christ, who has blessed us in the heavenly realms with every spiritual blessing in Christ.  For he chose us in him before the creation of the world to be holy and blameless in his sight. In love he predestined us to be adopted as his sons through Jesus Christ, in accordance with his pleasure and will--to the praise of his glorious grace, which he has freely given us in the One he loves.  In him we have redemption through his blood, the forgiveness of sins, in accordance with the riches of God's grace that he lavished on us with all wisdom and understanding.  (Ephesians 1:3-8)

I can do everything through him who gives me strength. (Philippians 4:13)

As you come to him, the living Stone--rejected by men but chosen by God and precious to him-- you also, like living stones, are being built into a spiritual house to be a holy priesthood, offering spiritual sacrifices acceptable to God through Jesus Christ. 6 For in Scripture it says: "See, I lay a stone in Zion, a chosen and precious cornerstone, and the one who trusts in him will never be put to shame."   (1 Peter 2:4)

## CHAPTER TWELVE

## The "it" of Persecution

**DEFINITION:**  Persecution is the act of subjecting someone to cruel and unfair treatment because of their ethnic origin, political views, or religious beliefs.  The biblical definition includes harassing, punishing, oppressing, or even killing those who serve God and refuse to deny Him.

## FACTS ABOUT PERSECUTION:

**The targets of persecution.**  The Bible reveals that true believers--those who proclaim God's Word and live by His commandments--are the targets of persecution.

**All who live godly will suffer persecution**.  The Apostle Paul warned: *"In fact, everyone who wants to live a godly life in Christ Jesus will be persecuted" (2 Timothy 3:12).*

**Reasons for persecution** include misunderstanding, jealousy, revenge, opposition, hatred of God and His Word, and Satanically-inspired motives.

**The root causes of persecution in a biblical sense** are wicked men who are motivated by Satanic powers to oppose God, His Word, all that is good, and believers who choose to follow the Lord.  The world hates believers because they are not of this world (John 17:14-18).

**You are actually blessed when you are persecuted**.  Matthew 5:11-12 says:  *"Blessed are you when people insult you, persecute you and falsely say all kinds of evil against you because of me. Rejoice and be glad, because great is your reward in heaven, for in the same way they persecuted the prophets who were before you."*

## DEALING WITH PERSECUTION:

**Pray that you will be delivered from persecution**.  "Deliver us from evil" is part of the model prayer (Matthew 6:13).  Paul said to *"...pray that we may be delivered from wicked and evil men, for not everyone has faith" (2 Thessalonians 3:2).*  David prayed *"save and deliver me from all who pursue me" (Psalm 7:1).*

**Forgive those who persecute you.**  You must extend to those who persecute you the same forgiveness that you have received (Matthew 6:12).

**Love those who persecute you.**  Jesus said, *"You have heard that it was said, 'Love your neighbor and hate your enemy.' But I tell you: Love your enemies..."(Matthew 5:43).*

**Pray for your enemies.**  Jesus said: *"...pray for those who persecute you, that you may be sons of your Father in heaven" (Matthew 5:44-45).*  You are to pray blessings over those who persecute you (Romans 12:14).

**Know that nothing can separate you from God's love**--not even persecution or death (Romans 8:35-39).

**Keep your focus on eternity**.  If you suffer with Him and in His behalf, you will be glorified with Him (Romans 8:16-18)

**Know that God's grace is sufficient.**  No matter what you suffer, His grace is sufficient (2 Corinthians 12:9-10).  You will have sufficient grace to help you in times of need (Hebrews 4:16).

**Do not back down.**  If you are suffering because of your Christian witness, do not back down. The disciples suffered in this way, but they determined to continue to minister the Gospel and to obey God rather than man (Acts 4:18-20; 5:28-29).

## WHAT GOD'S WORD SAYS ABOUT PERSECUTION:

O Lord my God, I take refuge in you; save and deliver me from all who pursue me. (Psalm 7:1)

Blessed are those who are persecuted because of righteousness, for theirs is the kingdom of heaven. Blessed are you when people insult you, persecute you and falsely say all kinds of evil against you because of me. Rejoice and be glad, because great is your reward in heaven, for in the same way they persecuted the prophets who were before you.  (Matthew 5:10-12)

You have heard that it was said, 'Love your neighbor and hate your enemy.' But I tell you: Love your enemies and pray for those who persecute you, that you may be sons of your Father in heaven.  (Matthew 5:43-45)

Forgive us our debts, as we also have forgiven our debtors.   (Matthew 6:12)

But before all this, they will lay hands on you and persecute you. They will deliver you to synagogues and prisons, and you will be brought before kings and governors, and all on account of my name. This will result in your being witnesses to them.  But make up your mind not to worry beforehand how you will defend yourselves.  For I will give you words and wisdom that none of your adversaries will be able to resist or contradict.  You will be betrayed even by parents, brothers, relatives and friends, and they will put some of you to death. All men will hate you because of me.  But not a hair of your head will perish.  By standing firm, you will gain life. (Luke 21:12-19)

If the world hates you, keep in mind that it hated me first.  If you belonged to the world, it would love you as its own. As it is, you do not belong to the world, but I have chosen you out of the world. That is why the world hates you.  Remember the words I spoke to you: 'No servant is greater than his master.' If they persecuted me, they will persecute you also. If they obeyed my teaching, they will obey yours also.  They will treat you this way because of my name, for they do not know the One who sent me (John 15:18-21)

All this I have told you so that you will not go astray.  They will put you out of the synagogue; in fact, a time is coming when anyone who kills you will think he is offering a service to God.

They will do such things because they have not known the Father or me.  I have told you this, so that when the time comes you will remember that I warned you. I did not tell you this at first because I was with you.  (John 16:1-4)

I have given them your word and the world has hated them, for they are not of the world any more than I am of the world.  My prayer is not that you take them out of the world but that you protect them from the evil one.  They are not of the world, even as I am not of it. (John 17:14-16)

Then they called them in again and commanded them not to speak or teach at all in the name of Jesus. But Peter and John replied, "Judge for yourselves whether it is right in God's sight to obey you rather than God.  For we cannot help speaking about what we have seen and heard." (Acts 4:18-20)

"We gave you strict orders not to teach in this name," he said. "Yet you have filled Jerusalem with your teaching and are determined to make us guilty of this man's blood."  Peter and the other apostles replied: "We must obey God rather than men!"  (Acts 5:28-29)

They preached the good news in that city and won a large number of disciples. Then they returned to Lystra, Iconium and Antioch, strengthening the disciples and encouraging them to remain true to the faith. "We must go through many hardships to enter the kingdom of God," they said. (Acts 14:21-22)

For I consider that the sufferings of this present time are not worthy to be compared with the glory which shall be revealed in us. (Romans 8:18)

Who shall separate us from the love of Christ? Shall tribulation, or distress, or persecution, or famine, or nakedness, or peril, or sword?  As it is written: "For Your sake we are killed all day long; We are accounted as sheep for the slaughter."  Yet in all these things we are more than conquerors through Him who loved us.  For I am persuaded that neither death nor life, nor angels nor principalities nor powers, nor things present nor things to come, nor height nor depth, nor any other created thing, shall be able to separate us from the love of God which is in Christ Jesus our Lord.  (Romans 8:35-39)

Bless those who persecute you; bless and do not curse.  (Romans 12:14)

We are hard pressed on every side, but not crushed; perplexed, but not in despair; persecuted, but not abandoned; struck down, but not destroyed. (2 Corinthians 4:8-9)

But he said to me, "My grace is sufficient for you, for my power is made perfect in weakness." Therefore, I will boast all the more gladly about my weaknesses, so that Christ's power may rest on me.  That is why, for Christ's sake, I delight in weaknesses, in insults, in hardships, in persecutions, in difficulties. For when I am weak, then I am strong.  (2 Corinthians 12:9-10)

And pray that we may be delivered from wicked and evil men, for not everyone has faith. (2 Thessalonians 3:1-2)

In fact, everyone who wants to live a godly life in Christ Jesus will be persecuted. (2 Timothy 3:12)

Let us then approach the throne of grace with confidence, so that we may receive mercy and find grace to help us in our time of need.  (Hebrews 4:16)

By faith Moses, when he had grown up, refused to be known as the son of Pharaoh's daughter. He chose to be mistreated along with the people of God rather than to enjoy the pleasures of sin for a short time.  He regarded disgrace for the sake of Christ as of greater value than the treasures of Egypt, because he was looking ahead to his reward. (Hebrews 11:24-26)

Dear friends, do not be surprised at the painful trial you are suffering, as though something strange were happening to you.  But rejoice that you participate in the sufferings of Christ, so that you may be overjoyed when his glory is revealed.  If you are insulted because of the name of Christ, you are blessed, for the Spirit of glory and of God rests on you.  If you suffer, it should not be as a murderer or thief or any other kind of criminal, or even as a meddler.  However, if you suffer as a Christian, do not be ashamed, but praise God that you bear that name. (1 Peter 4:12-16)

## CONCLUSION

### How to Get Rid of "it" though Personal Deliverance

When you understand self-deliverance, you will keep yourself from being bond; you will keep yourself healthy, physically and spiritually and be free from spiritual pollution. Every day, you will enjoy divine health and will not be spending your money on drugs and hospital bills.

Sometimes, there may not be a minister who is anointed and knowledgeable about deliverance to help you. Sometimes, you can be heavily attacked and the next service is about four days away. What do you do? You should never allow evil spirits to reside in your life. If you lack adequate time to do a self-deliverance in the mornings, after your quiet time, then, when you're having your bath, you could do it.

Whatever the causes of our spiritual afflictions, there are several proven steps we may try to help ourselves find freedom and healing. If these steps do not resolve your situation, then perhaps it is time to ask for help:

Step 1 — Conversion

Deliverance from any level of bondage, or harassment (collectively called, "spiritual afflictions") cannot be achieved without personal conversion. Deliverance from milder forms of spiritual affliction may often be achieved by the various acts of personal conversion—Acts of Contrition, Faith, Hope, Charity, and Consecration. "Prayer Acts" and other prayers, with fasting, and various devotions are often effective to drive evil spirits away:

So humble yourselves before God. Resist the Devil, and he will flee from you. Draw close to God, and God will draw close to you. — (James 4:7,8)

The first step, therefore, is make up your mind to live the Christ-life; or if already doing so, to persevere in living the Christ-life. This internal conversion, which is a conscious decision and determination to follow Christ and all of His teachings, precedes all other steps to deliverance. Without conversion to the Faith in Jesus Christ and participation in His family, the Church, deliverance, even if seemingly effective for a while, cannot be successful in the long run. It is the *"Truth"* that makes us free (John 8:31b), not prayers, rituals, counseling, or personal will in themselves. It is the confrontation with Truth that sends the demons running back to hell. This is why the method of Deliverance Counseling we use is called a *"Truth Encounter"*. As demons are confronted with the Truth, and as we are confronted with the Truth, of whom we are in Christ, we gain freedom. The foundation of all truth is Jesus Christ, who is Truth (John 14:6). Without our Lord Jesus Christ, we can never know truth or obtain it.

Some people believe they are unable to make a profession of faith in Jesus Christ. In such cases the person should ask God for help—ask Him for the faith that will save, deliver, and heal.

If we are willing to accept the gift of faith from God, our Lord will give it to us when we ask:

And I tell you, Ask, and it will be given you; seek, and you will find; knock, and it will be opened to you. For every one who asks receives, and he who seeks finds, and to him who knocks it will be opened. What father among you, if his son asks for a fish, will instead of a fish give him a serpent; or if he asks for an egg, will give him a scorpion? If you then, who are evil, know how to give good gifts to your children, how much more will the heavenly Father give the Holy Spirit to those who ask him! — (Luke 11:9-13)

Sincerely ask God for the faith that brings saving faith, the faith of conversion to the One, that is Jesus Christ, whom who declares:

I am the way, and the truth, and the life; no one comes to the Father, but by me (John 14:6) .... Come to me, all who labor and are heavy laden, and I will give you rest (Matthew 11:28) .... I will not reject anyone who comes to me (John 6:37) .... [rather] take my yoke upon you, and learn from me; for I am gentle and lowly in heart, and you will find rest for your souls. For my yoke is easy, and my burden is light (Matt 11:29-30)

Step 2 — Repentance

Essential to growing closer to God in faith, devotion, and love is to repent of those behaviors, desires, beliefs, and ideas that are sinful. The definition of sin is much broader than most people imagine. A definition of sin:

Sin is an offense against reason, truth, and right conscience; it is a failure in genuine love for God and neighbor caused by a perverse attachment to certain goods. Its wounds the nature of man and injures human solidarity. It has been defined as "an utterance, a deed, or a desire contrary to the eternal law."

Sin is an offense against God: *"Against you, you alone, have I sinned, and done that which is evil in your sight"* (Ps 51:4). Sin sets itself against God's love for us and turns our hearts away from it. Like the first sin (of Adam and Eve), it is disobedience, a revolt against God through the will to become "like gods" (Gen 3:5), knowing and determining good and evil. Sin is thus "love of oneself even to contempt of God." In this proud self-exaltation, sin is diametrically opposed to the obedience of Jesus, which achieves our salvation (cf. Phil 2:6-9).

We must repent of our sin, but repentance involves more than merely "turning away" from sin. Repentance must also renounce all that opposes God and all that He finds sinful. This includes renouncing Satan and his ways, renouncing personal sins, and renouncing all that leads us to sin. Some of the common sins and situations that interfere with deliverance include: involvement in non-Christian activities like the occult; persistent situational sins such as living together without marriage or remarriage without annulment of previous marriages; maintaining improper or problematic friendships; illegal activities of any sort; and sins that have become habitual such as pornography, masturbation, fornication, gossip, lying, stealing, etc.

The three greatest stumbling blocks to deliverance is Pride, Rebellion, and Unforgiveness and all the things that go along with those three sins. Repentance of Pride, Rebellion, and Unforgiveness is required to even hope for deliverance. Repentance also includes the firm amendment to avoid sin, and the near occasion of sin, in the future. Repentance requires a *complete* turnaround of our lives, a becoming a *"new man"*, so that...

...you should put away the old self of your former way of life, corrupted through deceitful desires, and be renewed in the spirit of your minds, and put on the new self, created in God's way in righteousness and holiness of truth. Therefore, putting away falsehood, speak the truth, each one to his neighbor, for we are members one of another...(thus) do not leave room for the devil (Eph 4:22-25,26b)

Step 3 — Confession

With faith and contrition of heart, repentance of mind, firm purpose to avoid sin and that which leads us to sin, we must now confess our sins before our God who is a God of forgiveness and mercy. This is a critical step that we will discuss at length.

The manner of our confession differs, but within our respective traditions, confession is required:

If we confess our sins, he is faithful and just, and will forgive our sins and cleanse us from all unrighteousness. (1 John 1:9)

... if you confess with your mouth that Jesus is Lord and believe in your heart that God raised him from the dead, you will be saved. For one believes with the heart and so is justified, and one confesses with the mouth and so is saved. (Romans 10:9-10)

*"Confess your sins to each other and pray for each other so that you may be healed. The earnest prayer of a righteous person has great power and wonderful results"* (James 5:16).

This confidant maybe one's pastor or another minister, or a trusted friend. We must be careful when choosing an "accountability partner." Since we will be revealing very private and sensitive information about ourselves, it is critically important to trust whoever we choose as a confidant to be discreet and to keep absolutely confidential the information we tell them.

There is wisdom in presenting oneself to an "accountability partner." Personal accountability is upheld when we confess to another person whom may hold us accountable for our actions. Confessing our sins to one another is a powerful way to break the bonds of sin in our lives. It is much harder to confess our sins to one another than to simply say, *"Lord, forgive me"*. While God is forgiving, of course, it is the demands of personal accountability before another human being that brings our confession into grounded reality that strengthens our commitment to turn away from sin in the future.

Religious ministers, psychologists, counselors, and others including the Deliverance Counselors of agency, are also bound either by law, ethical codes, or contract with the client (or bound by any combination thereof) to keep private and confidential all that is revealed to them. In addition, those in the ministerial and helping professions are usually trained in the ethics, legalities, and culture of maintaining confidentiality. They are use to keeping private the personal information of their patients and clients. Friends, on the other hand, may not have such training and may not be use to the culture of confidentiality. Thus, if one's confidant is not a pastor, or at least a minister, psychologist, or counselor bound by law and/or ethical codes, take care to ensure the chosen confidant understands thoroughly that he must keep private all that he hears and may not discuss it with anyone, not even with his spouse.

There is a great psychological comfort in hearing the words, "I forgive you" or the equivalent, "I absolve you of your sins." Our Father in heaven understands this psychological need. Thus, in His great love for us, He provided a way for us to hear those words in His name. It is God who ultimately forgives sins, but God, according to His sovereign authority chose to delegate this authority to His validly ordained priests. This power was given to the Apostles in John 20:22-23 and was passed on from them to those whom they appointed.

Our Father in heaven also knows and understands our need to be a family and for the family to come to our aid when we are hurting, to offer forgiveness when we fall, and to provide healing and strength to help us grow in faith. God forgives you when you appeal to Him with your heart-felt and sincere repentance and confession. Follow the tradition of your denomination and always offer a prayer for forgiveness as soon as possible after sinning. Then, in obedience to the Bible, seek accountability by confession to a confidant to complete your healing.

Step 4 — Removing the Greatest Stumbling blocks: Pride, Rebellion, and Forgiveness

We have already mentioned that the three biggest stumbling blocks to deliverance is usually Pride, Rebellion, and Unforgiveness. These three sins distance us from God. To draw closer to God we need to give up our pride, obey our Lord's teachings, and forgive those who hurt us.

In Deliverance Counseling we help our clients through exercises to locate pockets of pride and rebellion and to rid themselves of these sins with the help of God through prayer. Forgiveness, however, tends to be the most difficult, partly because of pride or even rebellion perhaps, but mostly because of deeply emotional issues surrounding the circumstances of the hurts someone has given us. Whatever the causes of our unforgiveness, deliverance is not possible until we can come to forgive, thus we shall discuss this topic at some length too.

The following guide is rather long, but this step is one of the most important. One simple MUST deals with Pride, Rebellion, and Unforgiveness if deliverance and healing is to be permanently possible.

Pride: Pride is the essential sin that leads to most other sins. It is the sin of Lucifer that led him to rebel against God resulting in his expulsion from heaven and becoming Satan.

Pride is a killer. Pride says, "I can do it! I can get myself out of this mess without God and without anyone else's helped." No, we can't! We absolutely need God, and we desperately need each other.

Pride also says "I know the best and most efficient way and how dare others get in the way of that" or "How dare things not go my way" or "How dare some person or something get in the way of what I want to do." Impatience is a factor of pride. Other ways impatience reveals our pride is getting impatient when we cannot find our car keys, or when we are late to a meeting, or if someone is driving too slowly for us on the hi-way, or when the computer acts up and interrupts our train of thought.

Impatience is the sister to Pride because it is caused essentially by our desire to have things our own way, in our own time, and according to our own preferences.

Pride is also the engine behind egotism (thinking more of oneself than one ought) and behind false humility (putting oneself down to be less than what one actually is). Pride is the force behind resistance to lawful and appropriate authority — whether that authority is a parent, teacher, police officer, government, employer, or the Church.

Pride is the basis of thinking of oneself as better than others, being pompous, and having contempt toward one's neighbors, employers, other family members, or the Church and her ministers.

Pride can also rear its ugly head in more subtle ways such as reluctance to apologize when we need to apologize, demanding our rights merely because it is our right, being inappropriately unkind or rude, jealousy, being quick-tempered, moodiness, brooding over wrongs done by others to oneself, depression and despair, or demanding that we are right about something, when indeed we are right about the issue, even though the issue is unimportant or can be handled differently (this is a major phenomenon in marriages, families, and friendships — the phrase "We need to choose our battles" is an important remedy for this).

Other ways that Pride expresses itself include: by taking personal credit for gifts or possessions and thus refusing to acknowledge that we have what we have by God's Providence; glorying in our achievements as if they were not primary a result of God's grace and divine goodness; by minimizing one's defeats; by claiming qualities that are not actually possessed; magnifying the faults and defects of others or dwelling upon the defects and faults of others.

James 4:6-10 and 1 Peter 5:1-10 reveals that spiritual conflict follows pride.

Examine yourself for these and any other attributes of pride and then pray:

Dear Heavenly Father. You have said that pride goes before destruction and an arrogant spirit before stumbling (Prov. 16:18). I confess that I have not denied myself, picked up my cross daily, and followed You (Matt. 16:24). In so doing I have given ground to the enemy in my life. I have believed that I could be successful and live victoriously by my own strength and resources. I now confess that I have sinned against You by placing my will before You and by centering my life around self instead of You.

I now renounce the self-life and by so doing cancel all the ground that has been gained in my life by the enemies of the Lord Jesus Christ. I pray that You will guide me so that I will do nothing from selfishness or empty conceit, but with humility of mind that I will regard others as more important than myself (Phil. 2:3). Enable me through love to serve others and in honor prefer others (Rom. 12:10). Amen.

Rebellion: We often place our confidence in the flesh not only with the "I can do it myself" attitude but each time we assert our own opinions above the teachings of Christ. It is a pride and a rebellion to say, "I want to do it my way" or "I want to think the way I want" without regard to the ways God teaches us to go and to believe. This is an arrogance that not only can get us into major trouble but also forms a major vulnerability for demons to come into our life.

Rebelling against God and His authority gives Satan an opportunity to attack. As our commanding general, the Lord Jesus Christ says, *"Get into ranks and follow Me. I will not lead you into temptation, but I will deliver you from evil."*

The Bible teaches us that it is the will of God for us to be obedient to parents, to civil government, to the Church, and to the pastors who are over us. We have two biblical responsibilities in regard to these authority figures: 1) Pray for them; and 2) submit to them. The only time God permits us to disobey those in authority over us is when they require of us an act or acquiescence in ways that are contrary to Church Law, Natural Law, or Divine Law.

Being under authority is an act of faith; we are trusting God to work through His established lines of authority. The authority that God has ordained does not mean, however, that we are to submit to abuse from those authorities. In those cases where someone in authority over us is abusing us in any way, then we need to act in appropriate ways according to the situation — such as appeal to the state for protection and relief for civil or criminal issues; or appeal to Church authorities on some issue involving religion or our parish; or make appropriate decisions such as terminating an abusive relationship, etc. Whoever the authority, who is abusing, we need to pray for the offender and to forgive him; but we are not required to be a doormat or target of their abuse.

Some of the lines of authority mentioned in the Bible include:

- Church leaders (Hebrews 13:17; Matthew 18:15-18)
- Parents (Ephesians 6: 1-3; Exodus 20:12)
- Husbands (1 Peter 3:1-3; Ephesians 5:23-24)
- Employers (1 Peter 2:18-21)
- Civil Government (Romans 13:1-5; 1 Timothy 2:1-3; 1 Peter 2:13-16)

Examine yourself for any areas of rebellion (deliberate driving faster than the speed limit is rebellion, too, you know!) and then pray:

Dear Heavenly Father. You have said that rebellion is as the sin of witchcraft and insubordination is as iniquity and idolatry (1 Sam. 15.23). I know that in action and attitude I have sinned against You with a rebellious heart. I ask Your forgiveness for my rebellion and pray that by the shed blood of the Lord Jesus Christ, strengthened by intercession of the that all ground gained by evil spirits because of my rebelliousness be canceled and taken back. I pray that You will shed light on all my ways that I may know the full extent of my rebelliousness, and I now choose to adopt a submissive spirit and a servant's heart. Amen.

Unforgiveness: Jesus Himself discusses the seriousness of failing to forgive. He tells us that failure to forgive those who hurt us will result in our not being forgiven ourselves by God. *"Forgive us our trespasses (sins) as we forgive those who trespass (sin) against us"*. The *Our Father*, the Lord's Prayer, which most all of us know and pray, Jesus teaches us that God will be as forgiving to us as we are to others.

Indeed, how can we expect God to forgive us when we do not forgive our brothers? Consider the follow teachings from Holy Scripture:

If you forgive those who sin against you, your heavenly Father will forgive you. But if you refuse to forgive others, your Father will not forgive your sins (Matthew 6:14,15).

But when you are praying, first forgive anyone you are holding a grudge against, so that your Father in heaven will forgive your sins, too (Mark 11:25).

If you forgive others, you will be forgiven. (Luke 6:37b)

Forgiveness is not about emotions and feelings. You can still be hurting, angry and upset and still decide to forgive. Forgiveness involves a mental decision, a decision of will, an act of your free will, even though you may not "Feel it".

The true nature of forgiveness:

1. **Forgiveness is not forgetting:** People who try to forget find that cannot. It is an unfortunate quirk of the English language with the phrase, "Forgive and forget". In actuality this phrase does not mean to "forget" in the sense of not remembering what happened; of course, we will remember. God says He will "remember our sins no more" (Heb. 10: 17), but God, being omniscient, obviously cannot literally forget. "Remember no more" means that God will never use the past against us (Ps. 103:12).

   To forget is really "to let go". We need to *"let go and let God"*. We let go of the past, but more importantly we let go of the hurt. As long as we do not forgive, as long as we do not let go, we allow the offender of our wounds continue to hurt us.

2. **Forgiveness is a choice not a feeling:** Since God requires us to forgive, <u>it is something we can do</u>. God will NEVER ask us to do something that is impossible for us to do; that would be cruel and God is a loving God.

   Forgiveness, however, is difficult for us because it pulls against our feelings and emotional hurts. Forgiveness is not about forgetting our feelings or our emotional hurts. We often will not "feel" like forgiving, but we must forgive anyway. As the Lord Prayer teaches us, God forgives us "as we forgive others". But how can God require this of us when we have been hurt so badly?

   God does not expect your feelings and emotional hurts to be healed overnight. He knows and understands our feelings and our hurts. He is a compassionate God and will help us to heal over time, as we are able. What God expects of us is not an immediate emotional healing, but a decision of will to forgive, a decision of will to trust Him to take care of the offender and to heal us, a decision of will to ask God for, and to commit to, being healed of our wounds.

3. **Forgiveness is not letting the person off the hook:** Forgiving is about you letting go, but it is not letting the offender off the hook. He will still pay for what he did, either before the Law or before God or both.

   Forgiving is surely difficult for us because it pulls against our concept of justice. We want revenge for offenses suffered. But we are told never to take our own revenge (Rom. 12:9). Revenge does more damage to us than it punishes the offender. God's justice will prevail, no one can escape it. Never fear, those who hurt us will be held accountable, but we must let God deal with it. In order for God to deal with it, we need to let Him deal with it by letting go.

   *"Why should I let them off the hook?"* But doing that is precisely the problem — we are still hooked to them, still bound by our past when we do not forgive.

   To forgive does not mean letting the person off the hook; it means letting yourself off the hook.

4. **But you don't understand how much this person hurt me:** The problem is that when we do not forgive we, in essence, allow the person to still hurt us! The question is, "How do we stop the pain?" The answer is **to forgive**!

   It is important to understand that we do not forgive someone for their sake; we do it for our sake so we can be free. Our need to forgive is not an issue between the offender and us; it is between us and God.

5. **Forgiveness is agreeing to live with the consequences of another's sin:** Forgiveness is costly. We pay the price of the evil we forgive. We are going to live with those consequences whether we want to or not; our only choice is whether or not we will do so in the slavery of bitterness and unforgiveness or with the freedom of forgiveness.

   Jesus took the consequences of our sin upon Himself. All true forgiveness is substitution because no one really forgives without bearing the consequences of the other person's sin. God the Father *"made Him who knew no sin to be sin on our behalf, that we might become the righteousness of God in Him"* (2 Cor. 5:2 1).

   Where is the justice? We might ask. It is the Cross that makes forgiveness legally and morally right: *"For the death that He died, He died to sin, once for all"* (Rom. 6: 10). This doesn't mean that we tolerate sin. We must always stand against sin, but we must give the offender to God and get on with our life.

6. **How do we forgive from our heart?** First, we acknowledge the hurt and the hate. If our forgiveness does not visit the emotional core of our life, it will be incomplete. Many feel the pain of interpersonal offenses, but they will not

acknowledge it. Let God bring the pain to the surface so He can deal with it. This is where the healing takes place.

Do not wait to forgive until we feel like forgiving; we will never get there. Feelings take time to heal mostly <u>after</u> the choice to forgive is made and Satan has lost his place (Eph. 4:26, 27). Freedom is what will be gained, not a feeling.

7. **Summary of Points on Forgiveness:**
   - Forgiveness is necessary to have fellowship with God.
   - It is not forgetting.
   - It is a choice.
   - Letting the offender off <u>our</u> hook is what frees us.
   - The offender is not off God's hook.
   - God says, "Revenge is mine."
   - You must acknowledge the hurt and the hate.
   - Forgiveness means we are agreeing to live with the consequences of another's sin — which we have to do anyway.
   - The justice is in the cross.
   - Choice is between the slavery of bitterness or the freedom of forgiveness.
   - Forgiveness means not using the past against the offender.
   - Forgiveness <u>does not</u> mean tolerating the sin or abuse.
   - Why forgive? To stop the pain! As we live in unforgiveness the offender still hurts us!
   - The issue of forgiveness is between you and God only.
   - The act of forgiveness is for your sake, and for your freedom.

Think about the people in your life for whom you need to forgive, people to whom you hold bitterness, people who have hurt you or disappointed you in anyway, or for whom you hold any kind of grudge. Be sure to ALWAYS include your parents, siblings, spouse, and YOURSELF. There is always something to forgive in our families and in ourselves.

Record all the names you can think of on a sheet of paper and a brief note as to why you need to forgive them. If you do not remember names, list them by what you do remember, such as "the guy in sixth grade with the red hat". If you cannot remember why you need to forgive someone on your list that is okay; forgive them for whatever it was — God knows.

After preparing this list ask God to bring to your mind anyone you have forgotten. It is not unusual to forget, or to push aside from our conscious mind, incidents and even the names of people whom have hurt us. These hidden hurts and wounds need to be healed as well. Thus, ask God to bring to your mind any person you have forgotten for whom you need to forgive, for whom you hold a grudge against, for which you are bitter, for those who have hurt you, with the following prayer:

Father in heaven, please bring to my mind the names of any people for whom I have held bitterness towards, grudges against, or have not forgiven for the hurts they have caused me. Help me to remember all these hurts so that they may be offered to You, O Lord, and healed from my soul so that I may live the truly victorious Christ-life. Amen.

Add to your list the names of anyone God may bring to your mind.

Now it is time to pray...

The following prayer needs to be said for each person on the list for which you need to forgive. Do not go to the next person on the list until you are sure you have dealt with all the remembered pain.

As you pray, God may bring to your mind various offending people and experiences that has been totally forgotten. Allow God to do this even if it is painful. Remember this process of forgiveness is for your sake because God wants you to be free.

Remember also that by forgiving the offender we are not rationalizing or trying to explain the offender's behavior. Forgiveness deals with the victim's pain, your pain, not another's excuses. Positive feelings will follow in time; freeing you from the past is the critical issue now.

If you are willing to forgive for your sake, so that you can walk away from this webpage free in Christ, free from the past and from person who hurt you, pray the introductory prayer below and then pray the "Prayer to Forgive" for each person on your list:

Heavenly Father, I now ask for your help in forgiving all those people on my list. Although I am still hurt and angry with them, I know that they are your children and that you love them more than I can possibly know. For this reason, my God, I ask you to help me forgive them. I lay down all bitterness, resentment and hatred for this person and I freely choose to forgive them. Teach me to be more merciful, my God, and help me be always willing, just as you are always willing, to forgive those who sin against me. Amen."

Prayer to Forgive

Lord, I forgive ___________________________ for (specifically identify all offenses and painful memories).

May God heal you and bless you!

Step 5 — Know Who You Are in Christ!

In order to gain freedom, it is important to know who you are in Christ. Thus, you need to evaluate the concept you have of yourself, to acknowledge the truth about God and about yourself; about your relationship and ideas about God and about the manner of our lives.

We often deceive ourselves about our position in Christ and our relationship with Him. For example, we may say to ourselves: "This isn't going to work" or "I wish I could believe this but I can't" or perhaps even more direct deceptions or denials concerning the promises of God for His children. Areas of deception that we may have include:

1. **Self-Deception** (telling ourselves things that are not true)

- o Listening to God's words but thinking we do not have to do it (Ja 1:22; 4:17)
- o Thinking we have no sin or do not sin (1 Jn 1:8)
- o Thinking that we are something when we are not (Gal 6:3)
- o Believing that we will not reap what we sow (Gal 6:7)
- o Thinking we are wise and sophisticated in the 21st century (1 Cor 3:18, 19)
- o Believing that the unrighteous will reach heaven (1 Cor 6:9)
- o Thinking we can associate with bad company and not be corrupted (1 Cor 15:33)

2. **Self-Defense** (defending ourselves instead of trusting Christ)
   - o Denial (conscious or subconscious)
   - o Fantasy (escape from the real world)
   - o Emotional insulation (withdraw to avoid rejection)
   - o Regression (reverting back to a less threatening time in the past)
   - o Displacement (taking out frustrations on others)
   - o Projection (blaming others or accusing others of things we ourselves have done)
   - o Rationalization (defending self though verbal excursion)

To counter these and other deceptions we tell ourselves we need to exercise faith. Faith is the response to Truth and believing the truth is a CHOICE (not a feeling). If we say, "I want to believe God, but I just can't," then we are deceiving ourselves. Of course, we can believe God. We know that God does not lie. Faith is something we DECIDE to do; it is not something we FEEL like doing. Believing the truth does not make it true; rather it is TRUE, therefore we believe it.

Examine yourself and how you may deceive yourself with "self-deceptions" and "Self-Defense" mechanisms. The pray the following prayer: ...

Prayer to Know the Truth:

Dear Heavenly Father. I know that You desire truth in the inner self and that facing this truth is the way of liberation (John 8:32). I acknowledge that I have been deceived by the father of lies (John 8:44) and that I have deceived myself (1 John 1:8). I pray in the name of the Lord Jesus Christ, and since by faith I have received You into my life and am now seated with Christ in the heavenliest (Eph 2:6), I ask you Father to command all deceiving spirits to depart from me. I now ask You to *"search me, O God, and know my heart: try me and know my anxious thoughts; and see if there be any hurtful way in me, and lead me in the everlasting way"* (Ps. 139:23, 24) In the name of Christ Jesus I pray. Amen.

Knowing the truth about oneself, overcoming self-deceptions and the mechanism of self-defense that hide who we really are, includes understanding our faith in Christ. It is by Christ that our lives have meaning and substance.

The following prayer is the substance of that faith:

Affirmations

I believe that I am a child of God (1 Jn. 3:1-3) and that I am seated with Christ in the heavenlies (Eph. 2:6). I believe that I was saved by the grace of God through faith that is a gift and not the result of my own efforts or merits (Eph 2:8).

I choose to be strong in the Lord and in the strength of His might (Eph 6:10). I put no confidence in the flesh (Phil 3:3) for the weapons of warfare are not of the flesh (2 Cor. 10:4). I put on the whole armor of God (Eph. 6:10-20), and I resolve to stand firm in my faith and to resist the evil one.

I believe that Jesus Christ has all authority in heaven and on earth (Matt 28:18) and that He is the head over all rule and authority (Col 2:10). I believe that Satan and his demons and wicked spirits are subject to the Lord Jesus Christ and therefore to me in Christ since I am a member of Christ's body (Eph 1:19-23).

I believe that apart from Christ I can do nothing (John 15:5) so I declare my dependence upon Him.

I choose to abide in Christ in order to bear much fruit and to glorify the Lord (Jn 15:8) and to accomplish the work of sanctification that Christ began in me through the Cross (James 2).

I believe that since I am a member go God's royal family I have the authority, in the name of Christ Jesus, to ask the Father to command the devil to leave my presence, as I obey the command to resist the devil (James 4:7).

I reject any counterfeit gifts or works of Satan and his minions in my life.

I believe that the truth will set me free (John 8:32) and that walking in the light is the only path of fellowship and freedom (1 John 1:7). Therefore, as a royal member of God's household, I stand against Satan's deceptions by affirming all the doctrines of the Faith and by taking every thought captive in obedience to Christ (2 Cor 10:5).

I declare that the Bible and the Church are the only authoritative standards for me (2 Tim 3:15, 16).

I choose to speak the truth in love (Eph 4:15).

I choose to present my body as an instrument of righteousness, a living and holy sacrifice, and thus I renew my mind daily by the living Word of God in order that I may prove that the will of God is good, acceptable, and perfect (Rom 6:13; 12:1, 2).

I ask my heavenly Father to fill me with His Holy Spirit (Eph 5:18), to lead me into all truth (John 16:13), and to empower my life that I may live above sin and not carry out the desires of the flesh (Gal 5:16). I crucify the flesh (Gal 5:24) and choose to walk by the Spirit.

In making all these affirmations, I renounce all selfish goals and choose the ultimate goal of love (1 Tim 1:5). I choose to obey the greatest commandment to love the Lord my God will all my heart, soul, and mind, and to love my neighbor as myself (Matt 22:37-39). Amen.

Step 6 — Worship, Pray, and Fast

**Worship as a Church Family:** One of Satan's favorite lies, apart from having us believe that he does not exist, or that he does exist and is more powerful than he truly is, is that since God is everywhere and we can worship Him anywhere and do not need the "community of believers ", the Church family.

Although it is true that God is everywhere and worshiping Him anywhere is wholesome and good, it is false to believe that the Church is unnecessary. Since the earliest days of Christianity, communities of believers gathered together on the *Lord's Day* (Sunday).

Scripture is very clear on the subject of Church attendance and on how our submission to its authority is not only good but required. The Church, its leaders and members, are the Mystical Body of Christ here on Earth. To disobey the teachings of the Church as it relates to faith and morals is to disobey the teachings of Christ. To not attend church is also disobedience to Christ.

Paul admonishes those who do not come to Church in Hebrews 10:19-25:

Therefore, brothers, since through the blood of Jesus we have confidence of entrance into the sanctuary by the new and living way he opened for us through the veil, that is, his flesh, and since we have "a great priest over the house of God," let us approach with a sincere heart and in absolute trust, with our hearts sprinkled clean from an evil conscience and our bodies washed in pure water. Let us hold unwaveringly to our confession that gives us hope, for he who made the promise is trustworthy. We must consider how to rouse one another to love and good works. We should not stay away from our assembly, as is the custom of some, but encourage one another, and this all the more as you see the day drawing near.

Hebrews 13:17

Obey your leaders and submit to them; for they are keeping watch over your souls, as men who will have to give account. Let them do this joyfully, and not sadly, for that would be of no advantage to you.

Worship and prayer together as a family, prayer meetings, adoration, and other corporate settings, and in the privacy of the family at home is critical in developing spiritual health for the family and each family member. Such family devotion forms the foundation for all that each family does away from home in the world of school, work, and society.

Prayer is so important both in the family context and individually. It is important not just because prayer is something a Christian ought to do, but because prayer is communication.

The more we depend on God, the closer He is to us and we are to Him. Aligning ourselves with God, communicating with Him at all times and in all situations and personal decisions will unite our hearts to His. A heart united to the Creator will overflow with graces and blessings.

**Prayer and Spiritual Warfare:** In addition, a healthy prayer life destroys strongholds that demons may have in our lives and in our hearts. Without prayer we cannot hope to be delivered from spiritual afflictions. It is no secret —prayer, worship, devotion, and living the Christ-Life in all that it entails is the formula not only for deliverance from spiritual afflictions, but for living the victorious life in Christ.

When dealing with spiritual afflictions, however, some special prayer considerations may be needed. Scripture states that there are certain demons that will only respond to prayer as well as fasting: *"But this kind does not go out except by prayer and fasting."* (Matthew 17:21). If fasting can defeat even the strongest of fallen angels, just how powerful is this sacrifice that we can make?

Spiritual warfare prayers are very effective in defeating the enemy and drawing our hearts closer to God.

Step 7 — Live the Faith and Remain Faithful

Along with all the advice and recommendations of the first six steps, our healing and deliverance cannot be complete unless we act upon our faith. Doing good works and charitable acts of love are a natural outflow of our faith and necessary to lead a good Christian life. It is not enough to believe. James asks and admonishes in James 2:19,20, 26:

Do you still think it's enough just to believe that there is one God? Well, even the demons believe this, and they tremble in terror! Fool! When will you ever learn that faith that does not result in good deeds is useless?

Just as the body is dead without a spirit, so also faith is dead without good deeds.

James calls a man a fool who does not act upon his faith in James 1:22-25:

Be doers of the word and not hearers only, deluding yourselves. For if anyone is a hearer of the Word and not a doer, he is like a man who looks at his own face in a mirror. He sees himself, then goes off and promptly forgets what he looks like. But the one who peers into the prefect law of freedom and perseveres, and is not a hearer who forgets but a doer who acts, such a one shall be blessed in what he does.

It is hard to live the Christ-Life, but we must try. We must not have a faith that is dead and useless. We must not be a fool and not practice our faith. We must, rather, live out our faith and persevere in the faith:

1 Corinthians 9:23-27

All this I do for the sake of the gospel, so that I too may have a share in it. Do you not know that the runners in the stadium all run in the race, but only one wins the prize? Run so as to win. Every athlete exercises discipline in every way. They do it to win a perishable crown, but we an imperishable one. Thus, I do not run aimlessly; I do not fight as if I were shadowboxing. No, I drive my body and train it, for fear that, after having preached to others, I myself should be disqualified.

Colossians 1:17-23

He is before all things, and in him all things hold together. He is the head of the body, the church. He is the beginning, the firstborn from the dead, that in all things he himself might be preeminent. For in him all the fullness was pleased to dwell, and through him to reconcile all things for him, making peace by the blood of his cross (through him), whether those on earth or those in heaven.

And you who once were alienated and hostile in mind because of evil deeds he has now reconciled in his fleshly body through his death, to present you holy, without blemish, and irreproachable before him, provided that you persevere in the faith, firmly grounded, stable, and not shifting from the hope of the gospel that you heard, which has been preached to every creature under heaven, of which I, Paul, am a minister.

And thus, let us be able to say, with St. Paul, in 2 Timothy 4:6-8

For I am already on the point of being sacrificed; the time of my departure has come. I have fought the good fight, I have finished the race, I have kept the faith. Henceforth there is laid up for me the crown of righteousness, which the Lord, the righteous judge, will award to me on that Day, and not only to me but also to all who have loved His appearing.

Persevere in the faith and let your life be a living Gospel for you shall thereby *"know the truth and the truth shall set you free"*

I have outlined steps detailing certain issues that we have found important in gaining freedom for a person in spiritual affliction.

1.  purify one's conscience by a good confession;
2.  Receive Holy Communion as often as possible;
3.  Implore the mercy of God by prayer and fasting.
4.  Recourse to specific spiritual warfare prayers applicable to the situation.

Final Thoughts

Repentance, forgiveness, acting on our faith, praying, fasting, receiving the Sacrament frequently, and all the rest we ought to do as good Christians are very good things and very necessary for this life, but more importantly for the life to come.

The advice contained in these Steps to Self-Deliverance, however, are not "quick fixes". This advice involves a lifelong commitment for anyone with spiritual afflictions. Freeing yourself from the bondages of the enemy and keeping them from returning requires this commitment to persevere in Christ and in the Christ-life.

There will be dry times. Your faith will be tested. Indeed, the demons may (and more than likely will) try to return. Scripture speaks of what demons do once they are cast out:

Now when the unclean spirit goes out of a man, it passes through waterless places seeking rest, and does not find it. Then it says, 'I will return to my house from which I came'; and when it comes, it finds it unoccupied, swept, and put in order. Then it goes and takes along with it seven other spirits more wicked than itself, and they go in and live there; and the last state of that man becomes worse than the first. (Matthew 12, 43-45).

Do not leave your house (heart) *"unoccupied, swept and put in order"*; rather be filled with the Holy Spirit.

We can never let down our guard. As a final instruction, remember the teaching of St. Paul in Ephesians 6:10-18. We do not go about our day without putting on our clothes. Do not go into the world with God's armor:

Finally, draw your strength from the Lord and from his mighty power. Put on the armor of God so that you may be able to stand firm against the tactics of the devil. For our struggle is not with flesh and blood but with the principalities, with the powers, with the world rulers of this present darkness, with the evil spirits in the heavens. Therefore, put on the armor of God that you may be able to resist on the evil day and, having done everything, to hold your ground. So, stand fast with your loins girded in truth, clothed with righteousness as a breastplate, and your feet shod in readiness for the gospel of peace. In all circumstances, hold faith as a shield, to quench all (the) flaming arrows of the evil one. And take the helmet of salvation and the sword of the Spirit, which is the word of God. With all prayer and supplication, pray at every opportunity in the Spirit. To that end, be watchful with all perseverance and supplication.

The purpose of all this information is to enable you to do a self-deliverance at home for yourself.  The process of self-deliverance is carried out in stages.  Let's go through them one by one.

**_STEP ONE:_**  Start with praise and worship.  You can sing songs to praise God and to worship Him.

**_STEP TWO:_**  Confess out loud Scriptures promising deliverance.  Luke 10:19, Ephesians 1:7, Romans 16:20, Revelation 12:11, Colossians 2:14-15, Galatians 3:13-14, Psalms 91:3..._2 Timothy 4:18_ says And the Lord shall deliver me from every evil work, and will preserve me unto His heavenly kingdom: to whom be glory forever and ever.  Amen.  You should memorize _2 Tim 4:18_.

**_STEP THREE:_**  Break covenants and curses to destroy their legal hold.  You pray a simple prayer like this: I break any curse or covenant working against me, in the name of Jesus.  (Simple prayers)

**_STEP FOUR:_**  Bind all the spirits associated with those covenants and curses like this: I bind all the spirits attached or connected to the curses and covenants I have just broken, in the name of Jesus.

**_STEP FIVE:_**  Lay one hand on your head and pray, Holy Ghost, cover me from the top of my head to the sole of my feet, in the name of Jesus.  Begin to mention every organ of your body; kidney, liver, intestine, blood, etc.  You must not rush at this level.  Lay your hands-on areas that the Spirit of God leads you to.

**_STEP SIX:_**  Then begin to saturate yourself with the Blood of Jesus.  You do this by saying: I plead the Blood of Jesus over me.  This must continue until you have a release in your spirit to stop.

**_STEP SEVEN:_**  It is now, that you can demand firmly, in the name of the Lord Jesus Christ, that any spirit that is not of God should leave you.  You demand it forcefully like this:  In the name of the Lord Jesus Christ, I come against all you hidden spirits and I bind your activities in my life.  You can no longer hide below the surface because I now recognize what you have been doing; release me, in the name of Jesus.

(**_If sickness is the problem, address it and say_**) You spirit of infirmity, I speak to you directly, get out of my life now.  I am redeemed by the Blood of Jesus Christ, come out and go now.  Go out with every breath by the power of the Holy Spirit.  I prevail over you, in the name of Jesus.

***STEP EIGHT:***   Ask for a fresh in-filling of the Holy Spirit and close the session with praises.  Self-deliverance keeps you from getting sick; it removes every evil seed of the enemy; it charges your body with fire.  It uproots evil plantations and builds up your confidence.  Every night before you go to bed, you must remember these two important prayer points.

1. Pray for cover with the Blood of Jesus. ***Revelation 12:11*** = And they overcame him by the Blood of the Lamb, and by the word of their testimony; and they loved not their lives unto the death.
2. Pray that the Angels of God should surround you. ***Psalms 34:7*** = The Angel of the Lord encampeth round about them that fear him, and delivereth them.

No matter how sleepy you are, make sure pray these two prayer points every night.  There is no reason why self-deliverance should not be effective.  However, if the person seeking deliverance is under stubborn demonic control or hereditary strongman and lacks sufficient faith or authority to defeat the oppressors or living in any known sin, the evil spirits will be hard to get rid of. right.

**One final word of caution**.  For a person to be delivered, he/she must want deliverance.  Self-deliverance must not be done because of pride, shyness, the fear of possible public embarrassment, etc.  Your motive for engaging in self-deliverance has to be pure.

REMEMBER: ***DELIVERANCE IS A PROCESS (((NOT A ONE-TIME EVENT)))*** AND THE LENGTH OF TIME IT TAKES DEPENDS ON SEVERAL THINGS;

1. The length of time the spirit has stayed inside a person
2. The strength and reinforcement of the spirit
3. The experience and degree of anointing upon those who are ministering the deliverance
4. The willingness of the person being delivered to be free
5. The knowledge of the Word of God and your level of hatred for sin
6. SELF-DISCIPLINE IS NECESSARY

Also, remember that bondage can be weak or strong.  A weak hold can be broken quickly, whereas a stronghold may take a more time.  You will not realize the strength of bondage until you faithfully and persistently work on it.  You must remember that a foothold can graduate to a stronghold if left unaddressed.  After this exercise, set aside some days (with fasting). DO NOT CONTINUE TO DO THE THINGS THAT CAUSED THE "it"! CHANGE YOUR HABITS TO AGREE WITH YOUR PRAYERS. AMEN.

# Appendix 2

## Exposing the Doors to Bondage

### Part I: The bondage

1. When did this bondage start?

2. Was there any unusual things that took place (or you did) when this bondage started?

3. If this bondage started when you were a child: Do you have ancestors who have suffered from a similar kind of bondage?

4. What kind of bondage are you facing? (Fears, depression, voices in your mind, mental illness, physical illness, mental torment, spiritual torment, etc.. Please be as detailed as possible.)

5. What are all the things that have impacted your life? (Parent's death, trauma, a certain situation that changed your life, anything that 'changed' you.)

### Part II: Your ancestor's background

1. Do you have ancestors who have struggled with similar problems or bondages?

2. Did your bondage start as a child and appear to have no reason to be there?

3. Do you have siblings who suffer from similar bondages or oppression?

### Part III: Soul ties

1. Have you been involved with extramarital sex? Are you attracted to an ex-lover? Is he or she a good/godly influence for you?

2. Have you been divorced?

3. Do you feel an unusual attraction to a past boyfriend, girlfriend or lover (who is obviously not right for you)?

4. Do you let anybody dominate, control, or make your choices you?

5. Have you ever formed a blood covenant with another person? (Blood brothers, etc.)

6. Have you ever made vows or agreements with somebody in effort to strengthen the relationship or commit yourself to each other?

7. Do you see any ungodly relationships in your past where gifts were exchanged? (Are you holding onto something that was given to you from somebody you had adultery with, etc.)

8. Have you ever had ungodly relations with any one?

9. Do you have any pictures in your possession of somebody whom you may have an ungodly soul tie with? (A picture of you with somebody you had an adultery with, etc.)

**Part IV: Relationship with parents**

1. What do you think of your parents?

2. How would you explain your childhood?

3. Where you close to your parents while growing up? If not, why?

4. How would you explain your relationship with your parents? Was it good, bad or very cold?

5. Did you feel rejection from your parents?

6. Was either of your parents overly passive or controlling?

7. Has either of your parents been divorced? Remarried? Are your parents divorced?

8. How would you describe your relationship with your siblings growing up?

**Part V: Rejection and abuse**

1. Were your parents married when you were conceived? Were you the right sex? Did your parents not want you, or want you to be different (gender, etc.) in any way? If so, explain.

2. Did you feel rejected as a child? As an adult? If so, by whom? Explain.

3. Did you face abuse? What kind (emotional, physical, sexual, etc.) and by whom?

4. Have you faced rejection from your peers, classmates, friends or those around you?

5. Have you ever been put down, belittled, or made fun of? If so, by whom? Explain.

6. If you have faced rejection or abuse, how did you respond? Do you feel you are still paying a price for it? If so, how?

7. How do you respond to rejection right now?

8. Do you reject yourself (self-rejection)? If so, why and in what ways?

**Part VI: Unforgiveness or bitterness**

1. Is there anybody you feel edgy around? (Don't like them, feel anything in your heart against them, etc.)

2. Do you have anything against anybody? In other words, is there anybody that you have a hard time demonstrating the love of Christ to?

3. Has anybody wronged you that you haven't forgiven from your heart (thoughts, feelings, emotions, etc.)?

4. How do your view your siblings, parents, coworkers, etc.? Do you have any hard feelings against them?

5. Do you make a habit of blaming yourself for everything? Do you obsess over your mistakes and feel unusually guilty for them?

6. Do you deeply regret things that you've done in your past? Could you kick yourself over something you've done in your past? If so, explain.

**Part VII: Personality**

1. Are you a very positive or negative person?

2. Do you feel confident in yourself? If so, why?

3. Do you have a low self-esteem? If so, why?

4. Are you domineering or controlling? If so, to whom, and in what ways? Why?

5. Are you an achiever? (A go-getter) If so, in what ways?

6. Do you feel that you are always right and that if everybody did everything your way, this world would be a better place to live?

7. How do you treat your children? Husband? Are you controlling, passive, etc.?

8. Do you like people to 'look at you' (as in receive attention)?

**Part VIII: Emotional health**

1. Do you strive to feel accepted? If so, how does this affect your lifestyle? By whom do you want to feel accepted?

2. Are you always stressed out? If so, why?

3. Do you feel hurt? If so, by whom/what and why?

4. Do you feel good about yourself? If not, why?

5. Do you feel depressed? If so, why? When did it start? Did your parents or grandparents struggle with depression? If so, then do you know when it started and why? Do you have siblings who are also struggling? Do you feel your depression is rational or irrational?

6. Do you struggle with fears? If so, what is it that you fear? (Fear of heights, dying, being hopeless, failure, never marrying, etc.)

7. Do you worry about things? What things do you worry about? Why?

8. Do you struggle with anger? Do you have a short temper?

9. Do you have any insecurity? If so, explain.

10. Do you feel any self-pity or feel sorry for yourself? Have you ever felt this? If so, why?

11. Do you find it easy to hate people? If so, over what kinds of things would a person have to do to make you hate them?

12. Do you have any irrational feelings? If so, what are they?

13. Do you feel like something is wrong with you?

14. Do you feel excessively guilty over anything? Is this a continual problem?

15. Are you very confused and forgetful? (Beyond the normal)

16. Are you aware of any emotional wounds that have affected you?

17. Have you ever been deeply embarrassed over something? What was it?

18. Have you been in or are currently experiencing very difficult (depressing) circumstances which may cause you to feel hopeless or depressed?

**Part IX: Who are you in Christ? And how do you see God?**

1. How do you explain your relationship with God?

2. Do you feel you aren't good enough to meet His standards?

3. Do you see Him as a loving father, or a dictator?

4. Do you believe that it's only by the Blood of Jesus that your sins are forgiven? Or do you feel you need to earn your forgiveness in any way?

5. Do you feel God's love in your life?

6. Do you feel like your sins are forgiven? Or do you feel guilty?

7. Do you feel excessively guilty in everyday life?

8. Do you feel that doing good things, you earn God's love and acceptance?

9. Do you feel that God is angry or upset with you?

**Part X: Spoken curses, vows & oaths**

1. Have you ever spoken something negative about yourself that has come to past? For example: "I'm sick and tired..." or "If I don't quit typing, I'm going to get arthritis!"

2. Has your parents, or those in authority over you spoken out a curse over you? For example: "You'll never amount to anything!" or "You'll never get out of debt" or "You're so dumb"

3. Have you ever made a vow out of anger? If so, what? For example: "I'll never let anybody push me around again!" or "I'm never going to be hurt again!"

4. Have you ever wished to die? Have you ever said it?

5. If you have made any vows or oaths, what are they?

**Part XI: Relationships**

1. Do you have many friends? What kind of people are they?

2. Do you have a hard time trying to meet new people or make friends?

3. Are you socially outgoing or shy? If so, why?

4. How would you define your relationship with your spouse?

**Part XII: Sexuality**

1. Have you ever had unholy sex? What kind? (Fornication, adultery, sodomy, with a child, etc.)

2. Have you struggled with lust, fantasy or unholy sexual thoughts? If so, what kind?

3. Have you been attracted to pornography?

4. Do you have homosexual thoughts and desires? If so, have you acted upon those feelings?

5. How do you feel about your sexuality? (Do you feel dirty about it, or do you feel it's a wonderful blessing that God's given you?)

6. Do you withhold sex from your spouse or are you fidgety? Do you enjoy a healthy relationship with your spouse sexually? How does he or she react?

7. Have you ever been raped or sexually abused?

8. Have you ever woke up and felt a sexual presence with you? There are demons that imitate male and female functions, and stimulate their host (a person) sexually (beyond the normal 'wet dream').

9. Do you struggle or have you struggled with masturbation?

10. Do you struggle or have you struggled with any other sexual related thoughts, desires, or bondages?

11. Is there anything sexually that you are ashamed of?

## Part XIII: Addictions

1. Do you have any addictions? If so, what kind? (Drugs, alcohol, smoking, eating, sex, TV, etc.) When did they start?

2. Did anybody else in your family (siblings, ancestors, etc.) have a struggle with any addictions? If so, what? Who?

3. Have you ever had, or currently have any sort of obsession over anything? If so, what?

## Part XIV: False religions

Examples of false religions: Buddhism, Hindu, Jehovah Witness, Mormonism, Christian Scientists, eastern religions, etc.

1. Have you ever been involved with any false religions? If so, why, when and how long? How do you feel about those beliefs now?

2. Have you ever been involved in any secret societies such as Freemasonry? If so, how deep were you involved?

**Part XV: The occult**

1. Have you ever shown interest in the occult? If so, in what ways? (Read up on it, dabbled in it, etc.)

2. Do you still feel drawn or attracted to the occult?

3. Have you had any interest in horror or thriller style movies or novels? Are you still attracted to these things?

4. Have you ever made a vow with the devil? If so, what?

5. Married Satan?

6. Worshipped a demon or Satan?

7. Have you ever put a curse or spell on somebody?

8. Are you aware of any curses or spells placed on you? If so, what? Who did it?

9. Dabbled with an Ouija board? If so, why?

10. Ever been a member of a coven (group of 13 witches)? Explain.

11. Communicated with the dead? Explain.

12. Told somebody's fortune or went to see a fortune teller? Explain.

13. Ever read your horoscope?

14. Watched or been involved in a séance? Explain.

15. Have you been involved or a victim of Satanic Ritual Abuse (SRA)? Explain.

16. Been baptized into a false religion or any other evil baptism? If so, what were you baptized into? When?

17. Have you ever had a spirit guide?

18. Have you ever been involved with meditation, yoga, karate, or related activities?

19. Were you or anybody in your family superstitious? If so, who?

20. Ever been involved in astral travel? (Out of body)

21. If you have made any vows or oaths, what are they? Were there any sacrifices or rituals that were accompanied with them?

22. Have you ever made a blood pact before? If so, with whom (including persons, demons and Satan) and for what purpose?

23. Have you ever partaken in automatic writing, automatic drawing or automatic painting?

24. Have you ever been involved in Yoga, transcendental meditation, or similar activities?

25. Have you ever sought healing from a spiritual source other than Jesus Christ? (New age healing, energy healing, etc.)

26. Any other involvement in the occult? Explain.

## Part XVI: Un-confessed sins

1. Are there any un-confessed sins that you have not repented of? (Usually something you've done, that you know is wrong, but won't admit to it. An abortion, stealing, etc. are some examples.)

2. Is there anything you've been hiding inside that you haven't confessed?

3. Do you feel excessively guilty over something(s) you've done in the past? If so, what?

## Part XVII: Cursed objects

1. Do you have any idols, occult rings, or anything that could hold evil spiritual value in your home? If so, what? Any objects that hold evil spiritual value must be destroyed.

2. Do you have any gifts saved from sinful relationships? If so, explain. For example, if a man gives a woman a personal gift during an adultery that needs to be sold or destroyed.

## Part XVIII: Severe trauma, abuse & disassociation

1. Have you ever been exposed to extreme abuse or a traumatic experience? Did it have a drastic effect on your emotional or mental system? If so, what happen? How did it affect you?

2. Have you ever disassociated or been diagnosed with Dissociative Identity Disorder (DID) or Multiple Personality Disorder (MPD)?

3. Are you aware of any alters (other personalities) that you may have? (If so, tell me about them)

4. Do you have a memory gap where you cannot remember a certain time of your life?

5. Do you have false memories of things that really didn't take place?

6. Have you ever been in a car accident or other traumatic situation? Have you ever witnessed a tragedy in real life?

**Part XIX: Weaknesses**

1. Do you struggle with any habitual sins? If so, what? Do you want to break those bad habits?

2. Do you struggle with any weaknesses such as lust, anger, hate, etc.? If so, what? Do you know where they came from or how they got started? Do you want to break free from those weaknesses?

**Part XX: Pregnancy issues**

1. Have you ever said something along the lines of, "I will never have children"?

2. Have you ever had an abortion or attempted one?

3. Have you ever had incest or ungodly sexual relations with somebody related to you? (See Leviticus 20:19-21, as this can cause a curse to land upon you which needs to be broken)

**Part XXI: Other things to look for**

1. Have you ever tried drugs? If so, how much, and how did it affect you? Why did you try drugs?

2. Have you ever thought about or attempted suicide?

3. Do you have any physical or mental disabilities, diseases or illnesses? Explain.

4. Do you want, and are willing to be delivered? Are you willing to give up those demon spirits and maybe make some lifestyle changes in order to keep your deliverance?

5. Do you experience unusual confusion settle upon you as you try to pray and read the Bible?

6. What kind of music do you like? (Please list all styles of music you currently enjoy, and give examples in each category you list, such as some names of artists and songs)

7. Have you previously enjoyed hard rock, metal, acid, alternative, rap, new age, or any other kind of worldly music? (Please provide some examples of artists and songs from each genre (type/style) of music you list)

8. Have you had any nightmares or weird experiences at night while supposedly sleeping?

9. Have you ever been in a trance or had an out of body experience?

10. Have you ever noticed time slipped right out from under you? For example, you look at your watch and its 7:00pm, then you look again what seemed like 15 minutes later and its 2:00am. This is a sign of a trance.

11. Have you ever touched or kissed a dead body? If so, explain whom and why and what happened afterwards.

12. Do you feel that you somehow have to earn your forgiveness? Do you 'wonder' if your sins are truly forgiven -- all of them? Are you aware of any signs of legalism or religious spirits operating in your mind?

13. Do you have any physical infirmities, sickness or diseases? If so, please list them.

14. Are you on any medications? If so, please explain.

15. Are you entertained by movies or TV shows which glorify death, murder, pain or suffering of others? Please explain.

16. Have you ever had any other kind of weird encounter with the spiritual realm?

Use this information to expose the root cause of the "it".

## REFERENCES

1. Gary R. Collins, *Christian Counseling: A Comprehensive Guide*, 3rd Addition, Revised and Updated, NavPress, Colorado Springs, Colorado. ISBN 1418503290
2. Beilby, J.K. & P.R. Eddy. *Understanding Spiritual Warfare: Four Views*. Grand Rapids, Michigan: Baker, 2012.
3. Boyd, G.A., *God at War: The Bible and Spiritual Conflict*. Downers Grove, Illinois: IVP, 1997.
4. Hiebert, P. "Spiritual Warfare and Worldview"
5. Stedman, R.C, *Spiritual Warfare: Winning the Daily Battle with Satan.* Portland, Oregon: Multnomah, 1975.
6. Pirolo, N., *Prepare for Battle: Basic Training in Spiritual Warfare*, San Diego, California: Emmaus Road, International, 1997.
7. Arnold, E. C., *3 Crucial Questions about Spiritual Warfare*, Grand Rapids, Michigan: Baker, 1997.1
8. Rita Bennett, You Can Be Emotionally Free, 1982 ISBN 978 0 88270 748 8
9. Rita Bennett, Emotionally Free, 1982, ISBN 0 86065 194 0
   Publishers, PO Box 777,
10. Tonbridge, Kent TN 11 0ZS, England, 1997, reprinted 2004). ISBN 1-85240-110-9. (Available in the US through the Arsenal Bookstore, 11005 Voyager Parkway, Colorado Springs, CO 80921.)
11. John and Paula Sandford, Healing the Wounded Spirit (Victory House, 1985). ISBN 0-932081-14-2.
12. Norma Dearing, The Healing Touch (Chosen Books, 2002). ISBN 0-8007-9302-1. Charles Kraft, Deep Wounds, Deep Healing (Servant Pub., 1993). ISBN 0-89283-784-5.
13. Derek Prince, God's Remedy for Rejection (Whitaker House, 1993). ISBN 088368-864-6.
14. Francis and Judith MacNutt, Praying for Your Unborn Child (1989). ISBN 0-38523-2829. (Available from www.Christianhealingmin.org, 904-765-3332.)
15. Thomas Verney, MD, The Secret Life of the Unborn Child (Summit Books, 1981).
16. Anderson, Winning Spiritual Warfare 1990 ISBN 13: 978-0-89081-868-8 James
17. Friesen, Uncovering the Mystery of MPD, 1997 ISBN 1-56819-062-7
18. Diane Hawkins, Multiple Identities, 2009 ISBN 978-0-9708073-6-6,
19. Restoration in Christ Ministries, http://www.rcm-usa.org/index.htm
20. Francis MacNutt, Deliverance from Evil Spirits, 1995, 0-8007-9232-7, Chap 17, pp 223-235 (best introductory material)
21. Daniel Ryder, Breaking the Circle of SRA, 1992, 0-89638-258-3 (an excellent book by a Christian counselor)
22. Margaret Smith, Ritual Abuse, what it is, why it happens, how to help, 1993, 0-06-250214-X (in depth information about SRA and MPD)
23. The Christian Bible
24. The following associations focus on trauma and disassociation www.sidran.org, www.issd.org
25. Pentecost, J.D., *Your Adversary the Devil.* Grand Rapids, Michigan: Zondervan, 1969

Dr. Paulette Douglas truly epitomizes elegance in living a saved, sanctified and Holy life, set apart from the secular world! Dr. Douglas is an ordained minister with the Pentecostal Assemblies of the World, an anointed national and international Evangelist, teacher and preacher. Dr. Paulette Douglas is renowned for the ministry of exhortation to the Body of Christ through deliverance, inner healing, salvation and biblical counseling at seminars, prayer clinics, crusades and conferences. She has established three churches and assisted in establishing many other churches, ministries and colleges as she serves on the Body of Christ for Jesus. Dr. Douglas was baptized in the name of Jesus Christ and filled with the Holy Ghost in 1977. She was called to the ministry in 1981, taught bible study at Pacific Bell for nine years which established the Radiant Life in Christ Ministries. She was the founder and pastor of the Radiant Life in Christ Community Church in Baldwin Park, California for nearly four years. Dr. Douglas retired in 1996 with full benefits from AT&T after 26 years of service. God introduced Dr. Douglas to the LOVE and HERO of her life, Bishop Robert T. Douglas Sr. They were married, the ministries merged, and she became the First Lady of the Jacob's Ladder Family, the Women's Ministry Director, the Church Executive Administrator and the Dean of the California University of Theology. Dr. Robert and Paulette Douglas are the proud parents of three wonderful children, Shakinah, Robert Jr. and Sondra Imani. They are also blessed with two granddaughters, Demi and Rob'Ann (butter ball) four grandsons, Dylan, Dominick Terrell, the twins Canden and Caden. Seven Godchildren and twelve God -grandchildren. Dr. Douglas is a graduate from Fuller Theological Seminary, Pasadena, California, Pentecostal Bible College, Ministerial Training Institute of Inglewood, California and Aenon Bible College West Coast. She has a Bachelors degree in Biblical Studies, a Masters degree in Theology, a PhD in Theology, Administration and a PhD in Biblical Counseling. She has earned certificates from California Christian Leadership of Orange County in biblical counseling, Zoe Christian Leadership Training Institute, Church Growth International, Seoul Korea and School of World Missions and Evangelism, Los Angeles. Dr. Douglas is formerly the Dean/Professor of the Inglewood Ministerial Training Institute of Inglewood, the Inland Empire Ministerial Training Institute, the Tri-County Ministerial Training Institute (San Bernardino, Riverside and Los Angeles counties) and the Living Waters Bible College, Rialto California. Dr. Douglas is presently the Dean of Colleges and Professor for the California District Council Aenon Bible College and Institutes, the Jacob's Ladder California University of Theology and Aenon Bible Institute CDC Extension Campus in Inglewood, California and the American College Theological Seminary International University (ACTS). All schools are fully accredited institutions for pastors, evangelist, teachers and anyone who has the call of God on their lives for ministry. Dr. Douglas is currently the CDC International Missions President and the past Church/Extension/Evangelism/Altar Director for the California District Council of the Pentecostal Assemblies of the World, Inc. Past Evangelism President for the CHDC Area 2 and has worked with the PAW Evangelism Ministry for more than 35 years. Dr. Paulette Douglas is the published author of the book series "Get Rid of It before It Gets Rid of You". Self-Help Instructions on how to correct and receive deliverance in every area of your life. Dr. Douglas portrays tremendous strength and endurance in the Lord by jointly sharing the vision and love for God with Bishop Douglas. Her primary objective in life is to be that "Excellent Woman of God, walking in His Divine favor.

**Books and Recourses Compiled by**
**Dr. Paulette Douglas**

**"How to Get Rid of "it", Before "it" Gets Rid of You" Series (12 Books on Self Deliverance)**

**Volume One-  Healing and Deliverance from Addictions**

**Volume Two-  Healing and Deliverance from Sexual Addictions**

**Volume Three-  Healing and Deliverance from Personality Disorders**

**Volume Four-  Healing and Deliverance from Negative Relationships**

**Volume Five- Healing and Deliverance Through Spiritual Warfare**

**Volume Six-  Healing and Deliverance from Negatives Attitudes**

**Volume Seven-  Healing and Deliverance from Success Hindrances**

**Volume Eight-  Healing and Deliverance from Tormenting Emotions**

**Volume Nine-  Healing and Deliverance from Spiritual Weakness**

**Volume Ten-  Healing and Deliverance from Salvation Issues**

**Volume Eleven-  Healing and Deliverance from Domestic Problems**

**Volume Twelve-  Healing and Deliverance Through Biblical Counseling**

**How to have an Anointed Altar Workers Ministry**

**How to have an Effective Prayer and Fasting Life**

**How to Walk in Your Grace as the Wife of a Minister, Deacon, Pastor, or Bishop**

**How to be an Effective Life Coach**